The Symbol of an Era

More than any other single individual, John Lennon—songwriter, singer, crusader—stood at the forefront of the musical and political upheavals of the '60s and '70s. Now he is gone, and an era has passed.

Working-Class Hero

From humble beginnings, the young musical genius parlayed hard work and a keen ear for the sounds of "today" into unparalleled success as a member of the world-famous Beatles. His voice is stilled forever.

Man of Peace

With his wife Yoko Ono, Lennon courageously sought an end to war and a renewal of human values through love. Together, in their art and in their lives, they strove to make peace a reality. But his life ended in senseless violence.

JOHN LENNON

This is his story . . .

THE
JOHN LENNON
STORY

John Swenson

LEISURE BOOKS NEW YORK CITY

Acknowledgements

Thanks to Barbara Mathe, Sharon Gude, Don Myers, Tom Ligamari and George Arthur for support and assistance in assembling this manuscript. Additional thanks to Grammy for the chicken. . . .

A LEISURE BOOK

Published by

Nordon Publications, Inc.
Two Park Avenue
New York, N.Y. 10016

A
HERO
IS
CUT DOWN

HE WAS, AS HE SAID IN THE SONG, THE GREATEST. He may have been kidding (after all, the song in question, "I'm the Greatest," was written for Ringo Starr) but it was never in doubt for the many fans Lennon inspired over the years. His loss leaves a gaping void in the world of popular music, a void much greater than that left by Elvis Presley or any other figure in the history of rock and roll. His death leaves a void in 20th century culture, in the worldwide quest for peace, in the sense that the children of the '60s still felt they could do something to improve the world.

John Lennon is dead, assassinated at age 40, and the world will never be the same. He had just finished a mixing session, working on future music projects with his wife Yoko, and was returning home to the Dakota apartments on Manhattan's Upper West Side for some much-needed rest when the killer struck.

"We had just finished mixing a new tune for Yoko," recalled Jack Douglas, who co-produced Lennon's last album, *Double Fantasy*. "In 1968 I was part of the smoke-dope, take-acid, riot-in-the-

street=and=go-mad generation, and I was listening to that (Beatles) White Album, and I said, 'God, what I really wanna do is produce records, that's really what I want and there's probably nothing more that I'd want to do than produce the Beatles, produce John Lennon.' Then after a lot of hard work, being a janitor in the studio and finally becoming an engineer then finally working with John in 1971, there was a communication, almost the kind of communication that a fan feels when he listens to a Beatles record. That was there when I met him. It was an instant warmth and we became very close.

"Then I started working with Yoko. Previous to that, engineers who would work with Yoko were running out of the control room when she was starting to work. I understood what she was trying to do and it was appreciated by both John and Yoko. We did a lot of work together. After the five years, I was coming back from Los Angeles and I got a telephone call from Yoko and she said, 'John and I wanna go back and we'd like you to produce.'

"My first reaction was 'Hallelujah,' not because I was producing the album, but because John was going back. I think after I hung up the phone I began to realize, 'They've asked *me* to do it.' "

"I didn't get through," Douglas says sadly about the night Lennon died. "After returning from the hospital I went for a walk, all the way down to Grand Central Station—I live uptown—hung around Grand Central Station for a while, and tried to make sense out of a completely senseless act, as best as I could. Because I had just left him at 10:30, we were feeling really up, we

Fans congregate at the entrance of The Dakota where John was shot to death. Some played tapes of the former Beatle's music; some came to garland the gates with flowers; all came to pay tribute to John Lennon.

were meeting again at ten o'clock in the morning to continue our work, we were feeling really glad that the album was gold, it was on its way to platinum. Yoko was receiving the kind of press that we had prayed for, that was making John very happy. Everything was going well.

"After it happened, I heard about twenty minutes later. Usually, because I only live two blocks from John, I ride uptown with him every night in the limo, but I had another session after that one, and while I was on my session I was told that John had been shot. I went over to Roosevelt Hospital and of course it wasn't long after that that I realized he was dead. And I spent the rest of the night in the streets. He meant the '80s to be optimistic. He wanted to tell everyone that ' it's going to be all right if we pull together'."

Within minutes after Lennon's death, reports began to filter out through the news media about the tragedy. At first it came over the wires as a simple story relating that an unspecified man had been shot. Soon after, though, the horrible details came out. Much of the country found out the tragic news from Howard Cosell, the anchorman of the Monday Night Football television broadcast. It was nearing the end of a boring but crucial game, and the outcome was still very much in doubt when a shocked-sounding Cosell reminded his audience that no matter what happened out on that field it was only a game. He began immediately to describe the news report about Lennon's death in a ghastly low tone.

Cosell reported that Lennon had been shot twice in the back in front of his home, that he had been rushed to Roosevelt Hospital where he was pronounced dead on arrival. Neighbors later reported hearing four shots fired, and further newspaper accounts described five shots. The killer had fired the shots at point blank range. Only one of the bullets remained in Lennon's body, while another was later found in the lining of his coat. After being hit, Lennon staggered about six steps to a security guard's booth in the entranceway to the apartment house, gasped, "I'm shot," and collapsed, bleeding profusely.

Yoko Ono, who was only a few steps away from Lennon but was not hit by any of the bullets, screamed, "Help me, help me," and a New York Police Department squad car rushed to the scene. As two policemen carried Lennon out to the car, eyewitnesses recalled that Lennon was covered with blood and was bleeding from the mouth. "Somebody tell me this isn't true," Yoko sobbed as they sped to nearby Roosevelt Hospital. But police officers James Moran and Bill Gamble, who had the sad duty of bringing Lennon to the hospital, probably knew Lennon was past hope when they brought him in and he was unconscious.

Dr. Stephen Lynn, director of emergency services at Roosevelt Hospital, confirmed the bad news. "Extensive resuscitation efforts were made," said Dr. Lynn, "and despite transfusions and other methods, he could not be revived. We tried to save him. We opened his chest and massaged his heart, but he was virtually dead when they brought him in. Significant damage had been done to a major vessel in the chest. There was a massive blood loss."

Within a few minutes of the announcement, crowds began to gather outside the Dakota apartments and outside Roosevelt Hospital. The fans outside the hospital soon knew they were mourners, but the ones at his home seemed unable to come to terms with his death. The fans who went to the Dakota came to share the saddest moment of their lives together. They numbered in the hundreds, some hysterical with grief, some numbed by the event. Many sang out Lennon songs in unison, burned candles, brought wreaths and flowers, but most just kept a silent vigil.

Dozens of media people were on the scene almost as quickly, anxious to get reactions from the crowd for late-night television broadcasts and the morning newspaper editions. One television interviewer approached a local policeman on hand for the crowd control effort. "He was just shot there," the policeman noted sadly. "I was still waiting for a Beatles reunion." Other local cops were also grief-stricken. They had liked and respected Lennon, and each of them brought up the point that Lennon had contributed $1,000 to the fund for bullet-proof vests.

Others openly expressed their grief at the scene. One woman named Eloise Johnstone said, "This is the end of an era and it scares me. I grew up with them. It feels like there's a death in my family."

"The Beatles changed my life," said Brian Sergio, who had driven in from Queens with his brothers Michael and George when they heard the news. "I started listening to them when I was 14 and, you know, in a whole world that was at war, filled with anger, they were the only people I knew who carried a message of peace and hope."

A musician, Robert Kinoian, agreed. "He changed my whole world. I can't believe it. I don't think anything could have been worse unless someone shot my parents.''

Another musician said, "On a musical level I can catalogue my life to Lennon's music, it's my guidepost. On a non-musical level, Lennon helped me define myself, what I think about myself. He defined what the ideal world could be and did it in a world that was far from that definition. It was music for change. And we changed.''

Others saw the gathering in terms of spectacle. One man appeared on the scene dressed in the costume of the grim reaper, clad in black and carrying a scythe. "There is a morbid fascination here, I'm embarrassed to admit," said another man. "We are the generation of assassination, and to be here is to be at Dealey Plaza, to be in touch with all the tragedies that have marked our lifetime.''

He said he'd come "to make some kind of a statement, I guess, but I know that in some disgusting way I also came here because I wanted that element of being at the scene. People our age have a sense of magnitude about events. You don't see just the ghost of John Lennon here. You see JFK and Bobby and Martin Luther King, all the people we look up to who've been taken from us violently.''

Some of the mourners kept an all-night vigil outside the Dakota. At one point the numbers had dwindled to about a dozen, but the next day more came, and by the following night their numbers had swelled to the hundreds again. Seventy-second Street and Central Park West was filled with mourners who stood in their lonely vigil, oblivious to the freezing rain that beat down mercilessly.

The fans put a heartwarming glow into an event so unspeakably tragic that the full measure of grief was arrived at only by degrees over the next few days. It had been these fans, many of them now well into their 30s and 40s, who had responded so totally and sincerely to Lennon's message of peace and love in the '60s, who had given life to his idea that the world could be a better place, just as he'd given voice to their certainty that the existence laid out for them by the cruel materialism of postwar American consciousness in the 1950s was an alien lifestyle that they could never really fit into. Lennon had shown these fans a better way, a life where dreams indeed became real if they were dreams of happiness and realization of human potential rather than just dreams of money, power and influence.

Those kids and John Lennon had shared a common vision through the '60s, a vision that had been crushed and twisted during the '70s and that Lennon had hoped to revive in the '80s. He had just begun his musical career again after a five-year hiatus. His comeback album, *Double Fantasy*, offered renewed promise that Lennon's vision could once again inspire a collective drive toward love and hope.

The magnitude of the grief generated by Lennon's death was surprising if only because so little attention had been paid to him during his hiatus from recording. Aside from an open letter to Lennon published in *Rolling Stone* magazine by rock journalist Dave Marsh, very little had been written about Lennon since his self-imposed retirement. In the letter, Marsh appealed to Lennon to return to action because his point of view and leadership were sorely missed at a time when rock music was struggling to redefine itself. The reader response to Marsh's plea was phenomenal, but there was no reply from Lennon himself and the issue seemed closed. What's more, Lennon's post-Beatles recorded works did not inspire the kind of sales generated by Beatles albums, or even by some of the other Beatle solo efforts. Yet *Double Fantasy* had indeed tapped the public's imagination strongly enough to be an instant success. "Yesterday, while we were working," said Jack Douglas the day after the murder, "David Geffen, the president of Geffen records, on which John's album is distributed, he came up and said 'Congratulations, it's two weeks out, the album is gold and quickly headed for platinum, and the single is going to be number one.' John was just thrilled. He'd been there many times before but after five years, he just jumped up and down like a kid.

"John was definitely one to play himself down. He didn't consider himself, 'John Lennon, Superstar,' but more like 'John Lennon, artist,' hoping that other people would try to understand what he was trying to say. He didn't take it for granted that people would just go out and buy this record. He hoped they would, but when it started to happen, the way it was, he was just thrilled, he was like a kid. He was very happy."

Obviously the public was eager to listen to Lennon's new message, and perhaps this explains in part why the reaction to his death was so strong. Still it seems incredible that so many people were affected so deeply by the news. New York City is a hard-nosed town used to assimilating, even shrugging off tragedy. The hard-heartedness many people have associated with this city over the years is really more of a thick-skinned stoicism that its inhabitants have developed after surviving two blackouts, numerous crippling strikes and a high incidence of street crime that has at times seemed like open warfare. New Yorkers have always shown the ability to smile in the face of tragedy, or at least to continue living in the best way they know how.

Only a few weeks before the Lennon assassination, a preacher's son from Westchester took it upon himself to ruthlessly cut down innocent people in the streets of New York in a vigilante attempt to terrorize the gay community in New York. It was a terrifying act of random violence that would have certainly all but closed down a town with less courage than New York has demonstrated over the years, yet people didn't choose to hide in their homes but went about their business, more cautiously perhaps, as if to prove that they would not be intimidated by such acts of violence.

On the day after John Lennon was killed, however, New York came to a standstill. People went through their daily routines, to be sure, but they were visibly shaken by the news, as if a close friend had died. Young and old, liberal and conservative, black and white, the grief touched everyone. People who had never heard a Beatles song outside of the Muzak renditions of "Yesterday" at their dentist's office somehow understood the magnitude of the tragedy. People who appeared untouched by the changes of the '60s walked about in a daze.

Policemen, firemen, bartenders, sanitationmen,

16

cab drivers—all mourned Lennon's passing. "It reminds me of when Kennedy got shot," said one cab driver whose balding pate seemed an unlikely residence for a Beatle haircut. "Except somehow this is worse. I identified more with Lennon. He was a regular guy—not a politician."

Elsewhere, New Yorkers mourned in their own private, and sometimes public, ways. Edward Koch, New York's mayor, expressed the city's deep graitude to Lennon for sharing his life with its inhabitants. "John Lennon profoundly affected a generation. His music and that of the Beatles was worldwide in its impact. He was an international figure, and New York City became his home. That made us very proud. Every death by violence is a trauma to society. The death of someone of John Lennon's stature intensifies this trauma. We mourn his loss."

President Carter said, "I know that I speak for millions of Americans when I say that I am saddened by his death, and distressed by the senseless manner of it. It is especially poignant that John Lennon has died by violence, though he had long campaigned for peace."

President-elect Reagan, in a startling contrast, suggested that Lennon's death wasn't so important and, almost as if he felt Lennon was upstaging his costly pageant of transition to a right-wing government in Washington, used the opportunity to make a speech against federal gun control laws. "Well, it's a tragedy," Reagan said unconvincingly when asked for his reaction to Lennon's assassination as he entered Catholic Cardinal Cooke's residence the following morning. Reagan quickly switched the subject into a fairly meaningless bit of official doubletalk. "We have to do something to prevent that kind of tragedy," he said lamely, adding that he has "never believed in handgun legislation," and suggested that the answer is "if somebody commits a crime and carries a gun when he's doing it, you add five to fifteen years to the prison sentence."

"The whole overall picture of violence in our streets," Reagan continued, switching to his familiar use of scare tactics to change the subject, "is something that has to be dealt with—we have to find an answer. If there is anything that the federal government can do, it has to be done."

Reagan's insensitivity to Lennon's assassination seemed almost calculated, and was sharpened by public knowledge that the previous Republican administration headed by Richard Nixon considered Lennon an enemy since he campaigned for peace, and had tried to keep Lennon from establishing residence in the U.S. by harassing him.

The gun control issue, which was last raised in such a serious manner by the late Robert F. Kennedy during the 1968 Presidential campaign in which he was shot, became an issue once more. "That gun was made for one purpose, and one purpose only," said New York *Daily News* columnist Jimmy Breslin in a television debate on gun control, "and that purpose was to kill John Lennon."

Meanwhile Lennon's records were selling at a brisker pace than they had during his life, even when his records with the Beatles dominated the pop charts, at one point holding the first five positions for highest record sales at the same time. Long lines of Lennon fans formed outside of record stores before they opened in the morning, and fans stampeded the racks when the stores opened, buying up every Lennon and Beatles album in stock in stores all across town. Bill Koenig, manager of Discomat III, said, "I sold 275 *Double Fantasy* albums in 11 hours. The only time something like this happened before was when Elvis Presley died. Many people came into the store crying."

Another store, King Karol, also reported phenomenal sales. According to the store manager there, who'd moved his entire stock of Lennon's new LP, "A popular album sells about 50 in a day, but this is incredible. We sold 200 copies of Lennon's album in one day."

Back at the Dakota, Yoko Ono was stoically trying to deal with the situation sensibly, gracefully acknowledging the fans for their care and issuing a statement through David Geffen: "John loved and prayed for the human race. Please do the same for him." Geffen, who was with Ono at Roosevelt Hospital when Lennon was pronounced dead, could only describe his reaction as "devastated. This is a great loss in every possible way. John Lennon was a great artist, a wonderful father and a wonderful husband."

Yoko further requested that instead of sending flowers, "please consider sending donations to Spirit Foundation Inc., which is John's personal charitable foundation. He would have appreciated it very much." Yoko signed the statement with love from herself and Sean and gave the address of the foundation: One Battery Park Plaza, New York, N.Y. 10004.

Spirit Foundation was set up as a clearing house

for donations for worthy projects in order that Lennon did not have to spend so much time paying attention to individual requests for funds from various charities and needy causes. It is a purely philanthropic organization—not even an officially listed tax shelter, as are most such organizations. The Lennon/Yoko Ono business partnership was extremely successful. John Lennon's assests were listed as 30 million dollars at the time of his death, and that represents only part of his potential wealth from investments and future royalties. His charitable gift giving was a sterling example of the beneficial uses of responsible wealth.

Last year Lennon contributed to Hale House, East Harlem Family Health Service, Covenant House, Society for the Prevention of Cruelty to Children, New York Foundling Hospital, St. Barnaby House, Salvation Army, Police Athletic League, WNET-TV, the police department (Bulletproof Vest Fund) and radio station WBAI-FM.

Most recently, the Spirit Foundation contributed thousands of Thanksgiving Day baskets of cheer for senior citizens and youthful residents of the Spofford House in the Bronx. In each basket was a personal note from the Lennon family, which read: "In this day of Thanksgiving, we are thinking of you and we wish you a happy life."

Perhaps the most impressive contribution, however, was Lennon's gift to the Hale House, a privately run institution for the care of children born to parents addicted to heroin, methadone and alcohol. Lennon had heard of the program and located the director through the *Amsterdam News*, whereupon he initiated a $10,000 annual gift to the poverty-stricken organization.

In addition, Lennon sent boxes of gifts and foodstuffs for each child in the program on several occasions. Each time John and Yoko packed the bags themselves, and were so interested in the children being cared for by the program that they sent their son Sean to play with the children there. "We have lost a dear friend," said Dr. Hale upon hearing of Lennon's death. "John didn't just help my mother and me, he helped the children—black, and poor. As he touched us, we touched others."

Nevertheless, well=wishers and mourners alike continued to show up at the Dakota throughout the day. The huge wrought-iron gates were covered with wreaths and flowers, some of which were bought from enterprising local merchants who sold them on the street. Other local shopowners, many of whom had known Lennon well, responded differently. One of Lennon's favorite restaurants, Hisae, is located directly across from the Dakota. The manager sent out free coffee for the mourners keeping vigil outside. "We lost a friend, too," said one of the waitresses carrying the coffee across the street to the fans.

At one point ex-Beatle drummer Ringo Starr arrived at the Dakota to pay his respects. Though he tried to slip out by a side entrance to the building, hysterical fans had followed his limousine and mobbed him in a bizarre reenactment of the days of Beatlemania. But Ringo was ashen-faced and oblivious to the fans, so stunned that he didn't even seem to notice when one woman reached in and stroked his hair repeatedly as he tried to get into his car.

Ringo had flown in from the Bahamas immediately upon hearing the news and refused to give a statement to the flock of reporters who'd assembled at the Dakota. A spokesman for Ringo did go as far as to say that he was "extremely shocked. He doesn't want to say any more."

In England, Paul McCartney, who fulfilled a recording commitment the day after the shooting, noted that work was the best tonic for grief and said, "I can't take it at the moment," when pressed by reporters for a statement. Obviously alarmed at the potential danger to his own life, McCartney hired a pair of security guards to patrol the grounds and screen visitors to his country estate in Sussex, fifty miles south of London.

McCartney went on to describe his reaction as one of "deep, deep shock." Lennon and McCartney had had a much publicized dispute which partly precipitated the Beatles break-up and continued for some time afterward but the two had settled their differences and become good friends once more in the last years of Lennon's life.

"John was a great guy," said his disheveled, pale-faced former partner. "He is going to be missed by the whole world."

George Harrison, the other surviving Beatle, was also described as "deeply upset" by a spokesman, and was so grieved he was unable to fulfill a recording commitment and spent the day following Lennon's death in seclusion at his country estate at Henley-on-Thames. The following day he said it was "an outrage that people can take other people's lives when they obviously haven't got their own lives in order. After all we went through together, I had—and still have—great love and respect for him."

Lennon's first wife, Cynthia, now remarried and living in Wales, also voiced her sorrow at the tragedy: "I would like to say how terribly upset we are at the sudden and tragic death of John Lennon," her prepared statement read.

"I have always had the deepest affection for John since the divorce and have always encouraged his relationship with Julian, which I thought was for the best." The 17-year-old Julian has been in Cynthia's custody since she and Lennon were divorced in 1968. "He was looking to his father for guidance," she said of the young guitarist/drummer who plans to have his own musical career. "Julian was hoping to see his father after Christmas. We don't know what will happen now."

Former British Prime Minister Harold Wilson, who suggested to Queen Elizabeth that she bestow England's highest honor, the Order of the British Empire, to the Beatles, said, "He gave the kids something to think about, he kept them off the streets and did more than all the forces of law and order could have done put together."

Perhaps alarmed at the near riot caused by Ringo's visit and to stave off curiosity seekers hoping to get a glimpse of other Beatle well-wishers, Yoko announced that she would accept no more visitors until further notice. "Her spirits are not good—the best we can say is that she is holding up as best she can," went the official report. "Her general wishes are to be left alone, she is seeing no one. She wants that they—that the world outside—respect her wish to see this thing through alone. She is working on a statement on what she wants to say—everything will be in that statement."

Yoko also announced that there would be no funeral, arranging to have Lennon's body cremated secretly and announcing that a silent vigil would be held for ten minutes on Sunday, December 14th, in his memory. "The place is all over the world, wherever people are at the time," said a spokesman.

An official statement was released two days after Lennon died on behalf of Yoko and their son Sean: "I told Sean what happened. I showed him the picture of his father on the cover of the paper and explained the situation. I took Sean to the spot where John lay after he was shot.

"Sean wanted to know why the person shot John if he liked John. I explained that he was probably a confused person. Sean said we should find out if he was confused or if he really had meant to kill John.

"I said it was up to the court. He asked what court—a tennis court or a basketball court?

"That's how Sean used to talk with his father. They were buddies. John would have been proud of Sean if he had heard this.

"Sean cried later. He also said, 'Now Daddy is part of God. I guess when you die you become much more bigger because you're part of everything.'

"I don't have much more to add to Sean's statement. The silent vigil will take place December 14th at 2 P.M. for 10 minutes.

"Our thoughts will be with you.
　　　　　　　　Love, Yoko and Sean"

*　　*　　*

24

The depth of grief over Lennon's death, and the repeated assertion that it meant the end of an era, caused a pair of his fans in widely separated areas of the country to commit suicide after hearing the reports. Michael E. Craig, a 30-year-old man from Salt Lake City, Utah, who grew up listening to the Beatles and Lennon and was currently unable to find work, was recounting his sadness about Lennon's death to a friend who lived in his apartment building, when he said "I think I'll end the whole damn thing." Craig produced a .25-caliber pistol from his pocket, put the barrel in his mouth and shot himself to death.

In Brooksville, Florida, 16-year-old Colleen Costello took an overdose of sleeping pills after leaving a suicide note describing her depression over "the killing of John Lennon up in New York." Her mother Jean found the note and told police that Lennon's assassination was the "straw that broke the camel's back" for her daughter. Colleen was only six years old when the Beatles broke up.

Yoko Ono interrupted her mourning to beg Lennon's fans not to hurt themselves in their despair.

"People are commiting suicide," she said in a telephone call to the New York *Daily News*. "It's hard. I wish I could tell you how hard it is. I've told Sean and he's crying. I'm afraid he'll be crying more. They are sending me telegrams saying that this is the end of an era and everything. I'm really so concerned.

"But this is not the end of an era," she went on to say. "*Starting Over* still goes. The '80s are still going to be a beautiful time, and John believed in it. I'm just afraid that instead of what John and I

25

believed in, people will start thinking of his death as the end of something. But it was just starting, and we know that the '80s is up to each one of us, and that should not stop. That sort of thinking is against what we believe in, and when something like this happens, each one of us must go on.

"John loved and prayed for the human race," she said, reiterating her first comments on his death. "Please pray the same for him. Please remember that he had deep faith and concern for life, and though he has now joined the greater force, he is still with us here."

Recalling those last moments before the killing, Yoko said "It was so sudden, so sudden. We had planned to go out to eat after leaving the recording studio, but we decided to go straight home instead. We were walking to the entrance of the building when I heard the shot. I didn't realize at first that John had been hit. He kept walking. Then, he fell and I saw the blood. We had planned on so much together. We had talked about living until we were 80. We even drew up lists of all the things we could do together for all those years. Then it was all over. But that doesn't mean the message should be over. The music will live on."

THE
BEATLES

LIVERPOOL, A SEEDY, SMOKY TOWN WITH A population of under a million people, is Northwestern England's greatest port city. Located in Lancashire on the banks of the Mersey River, its docks, which are over seven miles long, make it one of the world's greatest trade centers. Its proximity to Ireland makes it one of the key immigration sites in England, and thus it became one of the main funnels for U.S. culture into the British Isles. For this reason when seafarers brought rock and roll records back from America in the '50s, Liverpool became inundated with the stuff and its influence was felt strongly by the younger generation, who turned Liverpool into one of the world's music capitals in the early '60s. Mersey Beat, as the local sound was called, was the province of groups like Gerry and the Pacemakers . . . but the greatest, and most original sound to be identified with Liverpool was that of the Beatles, and it was John Lennon who did the most to coin that music.

Lennon's childhood was an extended period of sadness as one tragedy after another punctuated

28

John, aged nine

John and two Quarrymen pleasing the public in one of their earliest performances. By then Paul had managed to teach him a number of guitar chords to supplant the banjo chords Julia, his mother, had taught him. Their skiffle group was one of dozens in Liverpool. . . .

his earliest days. In fact, the tale of Lennon's childhood is the stuff of legend, a fitting preamble to the story of one of the most important figures in rock history. John's father, Fred Lennon, had to work the only kind of job really available to lower class Liverpudlians—seafaring. Fred served as a waiter on board ships, and met Julia Stanley while on leave in the dreary days before World War II. They fell in love, but saw each other only when Fred got time off in port. A little over a year after they met, Julia became pregnant and the baby was born during an air raid as the Germans bombed Liverpool during the Battle of Britain on October 9, 1940. In a gesture of patriotism, the baby was christened John Winston Lennon.

Things didn't go well for Fred Lennon. In the confusion of war time, his orders were apparently mixed up and he lost his ship as well as his job. He stopped sending money to Julia, and contact between them dwindled to nothing. Julia found herself alone, with no money and an 18-month-old child to raise. These grim circumstances led her to give up hopes for a traditional home life. She worried how young John would be cared for and eventually was forced to leave the child with her sister, Mimi, who lived in Allerton, a suburb of Liverpool. Julia's sister was married and could provide John with the family atmosphere that Julia couldn't.

At first John didn't realize he was living with adopted parents. Julia remained in the area and remarried. Mimi treated John as her own son. She kept him in the dark about his past. "I never told John about his real father. I just wanted to protect him from all that," Mimi said.

When John was about five, Fred Lennon returned to Liverpool. He went to visit Mimi and asked to spend some time with his son. They were to go to Blackpool, and, by Fred's account, "intending never to come back." They returned to Liverpool after Julia appeared and claimed that she wanted John. John was again left with Mimi where he stayed for the rest of his childhood. When things settled down, Julia visited him regularly.

John went to Dovedale Primary School. He was recognized as a bright but independent prospect by the headmaster. He learned quickly—but he got into a lot of fights. He became the leader of a group of classmates who spent their time shoplifting, fighting and generally getting into mischief. Among some of his teachers he got a bad reputation. Other children were warned not to play with him. John appeared to encourage the image. "I used to go thieving with this kid, pinching apples . . . I was the kingpin of my age group . . . The sort of gang I led went in for shoplifting and pulling down girls' knickers . . . As I got older, we'd go on from stuffin' rubbish like sweets in our pockets from shops and progress to getting enough to sell to others, like ciggies."

At home Mimi saw another John. From the age of seven he put together books of his own illustrated stories and poems. He read a lot and later remembered being very fond of *Alice in Wonderland* and other fantasies. This contradiction between the bad boy at school and the creative, sensitive youngster may have something to do with memories of his parents. His father was out of sight. When he would question Mimi about him she would avoid details and speak vaguely of his broken heart and inability to face returning. His mother would visit regularly and his feelings for her remained constant. Later he would speak of her visits and had this impression of one of them:

"My mother came one day to see us in a black coat with her face bleeding. She'd had some sort of accident. I couldn't face it. I thought, that's my mother in there, bleeding. I went out into the garden. I loved her, but I didn't want to get involved. I suppose I was a moral coward. I wanted to hide all feelings."

In 1952 John started at the Quarry Bank High School, a local grammar school near Mimi's house in Allerton. Mimi liked the idea of John staying close to home. She would be able to keep an eye on him. From primary school John had two close friends, Pete Shotton, who went with him to Quarry, and Ivan Vaughn. Ivan went on to the Liverpool Institute and would hang around with John and Pete after school. This continuing friendship would soon be instrumental in an event that would ultimately lead to the formation of a partnership that would alter the popular perceptions of the decade to come.

When John was twelve Mimi's husband George died. George had become John's friend. They would go out together. In arguments with Mimi, George would take John's side. Mimi thought John was very shocked by the death of George, but said he never showed it. Where Mimi took on the role of parental authority, George was John's compatriot. His loss further alienated the intelligent but confused adolescent. Around this time Julia started to visit more often.

"I started going to visit her at her house," John said. "I met her new bloke and didn't think much of him. I called him Twitchy. But he was all right, really. Julia became a sort of young aunt to me, or a big sister. As I got bigger I had more rows with Mimi. I used to run away and go live with Julia for a weekend, or eventually a few weeks."

John entered at the upper level of his class. With him went his reputation as a troublemaker. He made progress with his art studies but the rest of his schoolwork started to slide. He was very aggressive with his classmates: ". . . I wanted to be popular . . . wanted everybody to do what I told them to do . . . to laugh at my jokes and let me be the boss." To his teachers he was, along with his friend Pete, an undisciplined disruptive element. One teacher wrote, "Hopeless. Rather a clown in class. . . . He is just wasting other pupils' time."

This poor behavior continued. John and Pete saw themselves pitted against the rest of the school. Their alienation expressed itself in all the usual ways; more pranks and disciplinary action followed by lowered grades. Both Pete's parents and Mimi warned them of the trouble they were setting themselves up for. John and Pete would laugh it all off.

By this time Julia was seeing more of John and his friends. She was different from Mimi and the other parents and teachers. Julia talked their language. She would join them in their ridicule of people and things they didn't like. She encouraged their rebelliousness. Pete remembers Julia . . . "She was great. A groove. She'd just say 'forget it' when we told her what was going to happen to us.

We loved her. She was the only one who was like us. She told us things we wanted to hear. Like us, she did everything for laughs."

In his last year at Quarry, John had dropped to the bottom of his class. Mimi was worried that John was on his way to a life of menial work, petty thievery or worse. She went to visit the newly appointed headmaster at Quarry, a Mr. Pobjoy. He had gotten to know John initially through his reputation as a troublemaker. But, despite that, he was impressed with John's art work and thought the boy deserved another chance. It was through Mr. Pobjoy's recommendation that John got into the Art College at Liverpool.

John didn't demonstrate any real interest in music until the end of his days at Quarry. As a child he would try to imitate the popular tunes he would hear on the radio, but was discouraged by Mimi. He was given a harmonica when he was about ten, and he was able to learn a few tunes. Then, in the early Fifties, the popular music in England was of the smooth, crooner variety. Mostly from the U.S., this music was popularized mainly by vocalists from the big-band era of the decade before, the bands themselves having fallen out of favor and dissolved. There wasn't much life, as experienced by the children of the working classes, with which to identify.

By the late Fifties, things were beginning to change. The movie *Blackboard Jungle* was released. In many ways it was about the same frustrations and emotions that young people like John Lennon were feeling. The musical theme for this movie was "Rock Around the Clock," by Bill Haley and the Comets. This music, its beat, in conjunction with the images on the screen caused extreme reactions in movie houses across the U.S. and England. Kids everywhere were jumping to the beat, ripping up seats in their local theatres.

Another change, of a more local origin, was influencing the young John Lennon. This was the popularization of skiffle music. Skiffle was a somewhat primitive, amateurish, rhythmic, folk-oriented music with simplistic or nonsense lyrics. Its primary attraction was that anyone could participate. Knowledge of music was unnecessary—or talent, for that matter. A washboard for percussion, a string bass and a guitar were all that were needed. The guitar player had to know how to play only a couple of chords. Lonnie Donegan is best remembered for bringing skiffle to the public attention with two hits: "Rock Island Line" and "Does Your Chewing Gum Lose Its Flavour On the Bedpost Overnight?"

The single most important event in popular music that influenced John Lennon was the appearance of Elvis Presley in 1956. "Heartbreak Hotel" broke through the record charts in fourteen countries. Here was a young working-class singer setting the teenage world on fire with his music, his moves and his attitude. No smooth crooning. No saccharine ballads. These were sexually provocative, exciting songs that talked about things kids wanted to hear—but were not getting from any other popular source.

"Nothing really affected me until Elvis," said John. And at this time, like many others his age, John wanted to play the guitar.

Mimi had discouraged John's interest in pop

music, so John went to Julia. He thought she would be supportive. And, she knew how to play the banjo. Julia got John his first guitar—it was used and cost ten pounds. After taking a couple of lessons, he quit. He learned a few banjo chords from Julia, and soon learned his first tune, "That'll Be the Day."

Eventually John put together his own skiffle group from school. Included in the original group was Pete Shotton. They called themselves the Quarrymen. John remembered, "Our first appearance was in Rose Street . . . it was their Empire Day celebration. Put in the street they all had this party. We played from the back of a lorry. We didn't get paid or anything. We played at blokes' parties after that, or weddings. Perhaps got a few bob. But mostly we just played for fun."

The Quarrymen dressed like "Teddy Boys" and wore leather jackets, tight pants, and piled their greased hair up on their heads, like Elvis. They had a bad reputation and were used as examples by other kids' parents of the type of person to avoid.

The group was loosely knit. John was the leader. Other members would come and go. Often John would fight with members of the group. This would add to the turnover. John would stay. The other guy would leave—but John would stay.

During this time Ivan Vaughn, John's other close friend from the Dovedale days, was hanging around with John after school. He had no musical talent, but, being a friend of John's, he would occasionally play with the band. What Ivan did do was bring other players around to meet John. Most of these were classmates from the Liverpool

Institute. Some would be invited to play with the group. Most would leave after having a fight with John.

The Woolton Parish Church was located near Mimi's house. John knew some people there and persuaded them to have the Quarrymen perform at a church fête. It was here, on June 15, 1957, that Ivan Vaughn brought Paul McCartney to meet John Lennon.

They were playing outdoors. Paul was wearing a white sport coat and tight black pants. After they finished playing, Paul introduced himself.

"I went round to see them afterwards in the church hall place," Paul said. "I talked to them, just chatting and showing off. I showed them how to play 'Twenty Flight Rock' and told them all the words. They didn't know it. Then I did 'Bee Bop a Loo,' which they didn't know properly either. Then I did my Little Richard bit—went through my whole repertoire, in fact. I remember this beery old man getting nearer . . . breathing down my neck as I was playing. 'What's this old drunk doing?' I thought. Then he said 'Twenty Flight Rock ' was one of his favorites—so I knew he was a connoisseur.

"It was John. He'd just had a few beers. He was sixteen and I was fourteen, so he was a big man. I showed him a few more chords he didn't know. Then I left. I felt I'd made a good impression."

John remembers the meeting. "I was very impressed by Paul playing 'Twenty Flight Rock.' He could obviously play the guitar. I half thought to myself, 'He's as good as me.' I'd been kingpin up to then. Now, I thought, if I take him on what will happen? It went through my head that I'd have to keep him in line if I let him join. But he was good. So he was worth having. He also looked like Elvis. I dug him."

A few days later Paul met Pete Shotton on the street. Pete told him that they had been talking about him and would he like to join the group? Paul said okay.

John and Paul first performed together publicly at the end of the summer of 1957. The Quarrymen played a dance at the Conservative Club in Broadway outside of Liverpool. When it was over Paul played a couple of songs he had written. Up until this time John had been using other people's material, altering it as he saw fit. Not to be outdone by this new member, he started writing songs of his own. Though there was the element of rivalry, John and Paul started spending more time together, writing songs, playing guitar, talking about the music and getting to know one another. This was the beginning of the Lennon-McCartney signature that would thrive for the next twelve years.

Paul had a friend from school whom he thought would be good for the band. George Harrison was fifteen, but he could play guitar better than either Lennon or McCartney. George looked like a real Teddy Boy with his tight pants and long hair. His mother was supportive of her son's interest in music and let the boys practice at the Harrison house.

John remembers being hesitant about George joining the group, mainly because of his age. "It was too much, too much. George was just too young. I didn't want to know him at first. . . . George wanted to join us because he knew more chords, a lot more than we knew. So we got a lot from him. Every time we learned a new chord we'd write a song around it. We used to sag off school and go to George's house for the afternoon. George looked even younger than Paul. And Paul looked about ten, with his baby face.''

With this basic group they spent the next year together. George's guitar playing continued to improve. John and Paul wrote songs. They listened to a lot of music on the radio, learning how to put songs together by trying to reproduce what they heard. They practiced. Sometimes they got bookings at a local school or church dance. They always looked for players, especially when they got work. People would come and go—losing interest, or as a result of some run-in with John.

In 1958, Julia was killed, hit by a car while returning home from a visit with Mimi. For John it was a terrible blow.

John recalled, ''I was staying with Julia and Twitchy (Julia's second husband) this weekend. We were sitting waiting for her to come home. Twitchy was wondering why she was so late. The copper came to the door to tell us about the accident. It was just like it was supposed to be, the way it is in the films. Asking if I was her son and all that. Then he told us, and we both went white. It was the worst thing that ever happened to me. We'd caught up so much, me and Julia, in such a few years. We could communicate. We got on. She was great. I thought, fuck it, fuck it, fuck it. That's really fucked everything. I've no responsibilities to anyone now.

''We got a taxi over to Sefton General where she was lying dead. I didn't want to see her. I talked hysterically to the taxi driver. Just ranted on and on the way you do, just babbled on . . . I refused to go in and see her. But Twitchy did.''

John withdrew into himself. He became more abusive, to friends and strangers alike. Pete Shotton says, ''John never talked much about Julia or how he felt. But he took it out on his girls. I remember one of them shouting at him, 'Don't take it out on me' cuz your mother's dead.' ''

In 1956, Paul's mother died of cancer. John and Paul developed their bond of friendship through their music, which was augmented and tempered by this shared grief and sense of loss.

Lennon was enrolled in the Art College of Liverpool, but he wasn't attending many classes. He was spending much of his time with the band, practicing and playing occasional dates, or chasing girls. In his Lettering class was a girl he didn't chase. She was Cynthia Powell and she was everything John Lennon wasn't. She was quiet, somewhat shy and from a good home in the good part of town.

''I just thought he was horrible. My first memory of ever looking at him properly was in a lecture theatre were I saw Helen Anderson sitting behind him stroking his hair. It awoke something in me. I thought it was dislike at first. Then I realized it was jealousy. But I never had contact with him, apart from him stealing things from me, like rulers and brushes. He looked awful in those days as well. He had this long tweed overcoat that had belonged to his uncle George, and his hair all greased back. I didn't fancy him at all. He was all scruffy. But I didn't get a chance to know him, anyway. I wasn't part of his crowd. I was so respectable, or I thought I was.''

They met, properly, at a Christmas dance. Until then, they had not exchanged more than a few words. They started to go out together and eventually married.

In his first year at Art College John also met Stuart Sutcliffe. Stu was a physically frail, intense individual. He was a talented painter, knowledgeable in art history. John felt an immediate camaraderie with Stu and they became fast friends.

Stu entered some of his paintings in a nationwide art exposition and won a prize of sixty pounds, a considerable sum. Stu was interested in the band even before he became friends with John. He was attracted to the music and liked the idea of a group effort. He had always said that he wished he could play an instrument and be a part of a group. John persuaded Stu to spend his prize money on a bass guitar. The group needed a bass. If Stu got the guitar, they would teach him how to play, and he could join the band.

''Stu had no idea how to play it,'' said George. ''We all showed him what we could, but he really picked it up by coming around with us and playing on stage.'' Pictures from those early days show Stu with his back to the audience, embarrassed about his limited playing abilities.

By the end of 1959 the Quarrymen dropped their name, as well as their identity as a skiffle group. They were acquiring some equipment and getting louder, with a more pronounced beat than skiffle. They went through a number of names during this time, making up a new one for any given performance. It was under the name ''Moondogs''

41

that they had their first taste of professional life.

They won a competition and were invited to go to Manchester to be contestants on the "Carroll Levis Discoveries Show," a television showcase for new talent. At the end of the show, competing groups would reappear, play the opening bars of the song they performed earlier and the audience would vote by applause. The Moondogs did reasónably well, but because they had to catch the last train to Liverpool, they were unable to stay for the voting at the end of the show. By their absence, the Moondogs were ignored and forgotten.

In Liverpool, "beat" music was gaining popularity. There were many groups playing at that time in the various clubs and school or church functions. Band competitions and auditions were common. John, Paul and George were preparing for their important audition with Larry Parnes, the "King of British Rock and Roll." In addition to a drummer, they needed a new name.

"I was sitting at home one day," said John, "just thinking what a good name 'the Crickets' would be for an English group. The idea of beetles came into my head. I decided to spell Beatles to make it look like beat music, just as a joke."

For the audition they decided on the "Silver Beatles." Larry Parnes offered them a job. They were to be the second act on a two-week tour of Scotland. The headliner was a popular singer, Johnny Gentle. They found a drummer, one Thomas Moore, and prepared for the tour. Excited about their entry into show business, they took on stage names. Paul, romantically inclined, called himself Paul Ramon. George became Carl Harrison, after Carl Perkins. Stu kept his own name. John was known as Johnny Silver. They had a good time and they were thrilled to see "Silver Beatles" up on the posters. A postcard from Paul to his father reads: "It's gear. I've been asked for my autograph."

The return to Liverpool was something of a letdown. They were able to get some work, but as George recalls, "Scotland had been our first glimpse of show biz, a faint hope. It was a bit of a comedown to be back in Liverpool. We were lucky to get more than two dates a week. We were making about 15 bob a night, plus as much eggs on toast and Cokes as we could take."

After the Scotland tour they dropped the "Silver" and called themselves The Beatles.

As the Quarrymen, the group had been the house band at the Casbah, a local Liverpool club. It was located in the basement of a large house owned by Mr. and Mrs. Best. Their son, Pete, had asked to use the basement. He wanted a place where he and his friend could listen to records. As Mrs. Best remembers, "The original idea was that it would be their den. That developed into the idea of making it into a coffee club just for teenagers."

The Quarrymen opened the club and were a big success. They played regularly until a dispute over money resulted in their leaving. Pete Best had become a drummer and formed his own group, the Blackjacks, who took over at the Casbah when the Quarrymen left. The Casbah continued its success.

Another local club owner, Alan Williams, had been expanding his interests beyond his club, the Jackaranda. He had worked with Larry Parnes on the Scotland tour, and had made contact with some people in London. On a trip to London,

Williams met Bruno Koschmeider. Koschmeider was looking for English groups to book in his club in Hamburg, Germany. Williams suggested a group he had worked with, Derry and the Seniors. An agreement was reached, and they became the first group from Liverpool to play in Hamburg. The German was pleased and asked Williams if he could find him another group. Williams approached the Beatles.

Everyone was excited with the prospects, but each had to receive family permission in order to go. Mrs. Harrison didn't try to stop George from going, but she was worried. George was only seventeen, and she had heard stories about how rough Hamburg could be. Paul's father was harder to convince, but eventually said yes. Mimi was something else. She had banned John from playing guitar at home and from playing in the group. John had lied about his playing, and covered up his activities. She never realized how involved he had become with playing and the group. She thought he was applying himself to school. When John announced his plans, Mimi was quite shocked but could do little to stop him.

Pete Best left school in the summer of 1960. The Blackjacks had broken up and he was left with nothing to do. In August, Paul McCartney approached him. "Paul said, had I still got any drums. I told him that I had just got a complete new kit. I was very proud of that. He said they'd got a job in Hamburg and would I be interested in being their drummer? I said yes. I'd always liked them very much. They said I'd get 15 pounds a week, which was a lot.

"I went down to Alan Williams' club, the

Jackaranda. I met Stu for the first time. I had an audition. I blasted off a few numbers and they all said fine, you can come to Hamburg with us.''

The job in Hamburg would prove to be their big step from amateurs to professionals. They were in a foreign country, cut off from family and friends, playing rock and roll for a living. Hamburg was a hard learning experience.

They were to play at Koschmeider's club, the Kaiserkeller, but ended up at a roach-infested dive, called the Indra Club. In Liverpool the standard set was one hour. Here, they were expected to play for eight hours a night. They were put up in a building that housed a movie theater. After playing all night they would fall over, exhausted, only to be blasted awake in a few short hours by the soundtrack of German movies. They started using amphetamines to keep going. This cycle of marathon playing in an alien environment and the lack of regular sleep affected everyone. John and Stu got more outrageous on stage. Jumping around, falling over, screaming insults in English, they made a rowdy sight. The sailors and hookers who made up most of the audience loved it.

After eight weeks at the Indra, the club folded. The Beatles moved to the Kaiserkeller, where they switched off hour-long sets with a group called Rory Storm and the Hurricanes. By this time they were heavily into rock and roll. They would play Elvis, Little Richard, Chuck Berry and whatever else was yelled to them from the audience. The American and English sailors wanted to hear Country and Western songs, like those by Hank Williams. The drummer for the Hurricanes was a fan of C &W and would join in on requests. The drummer was Richard Starkey, whose stage name was Ringo Starr. He soon became friends with the band.

As time went on, the Kaiserkeller began to attract students and other bohemian types in addition to the usual sailors. Klaus Voormann, a student, stumbled in one night and was excited by what he saw and heard. He started bringing friends with him. One was a young woman named Astrid Kirchherr. She took an immediate liking to the group and invited them to her house for meals, took pictures of them and gave them haircuts. Stu was attracted to Astrid and they started dating.

They were doing well and decided to try to get work at a better, higher-paying job. They approached Peter Eckhorn, the manager of the Top Ten Club. After auditioning, they were offered the job. Things looked as if they were starting to take off.

But, events turned sour. George, who was too young to work legally in Germany, was found out and deported. George, Paul and Pete Best were implicated in a suspicious fire. After being arrested they, too, were deported. John soon followed.

Their return to Liverpool was not all that bad. They were a much better band than when they left. Well practiced and with tight vocals, they were soon getting a lot of work. They played the Casbah, the Cavern and other local club and halls in the area. And they started attracting more fans.

After a year of successful dates in Liverpool, the Beatles returned for a short run at the Top Ten Club. While on this trip to Hamburg, they made their first record backing up a local singer,

*Clubs Beatles played at in
Hamburg as well as Liverpool were sometimes
stripper "showcases" where the girls took it all off to
the constant beat of Beatle music. . . .*

Tony Sheridan. The record was a version of "My Bonnie," a traditional English song. Around this time they also began to wear their hair in what would be known as the Beatle Cut. There is some discrepancy as to its origins. Astrid and her artist friends are sometimes credited with introducing it to the band. There was a similar style popular at the universities. It was called the "Julius Ceasar."

When they returned to England, Stu announced that he was leaving the group. He wanted to stay in Hamburg with Astrid and study painting. This worked well for the group. Paul played better than Stu and would take over on bass, leaving George on lead and John on rhythm. Pete Best continued on drums.

Nine months after the Beatles returned to Liverpool, Stu Sutcliffe died of a brain hemorrhage.

Brian Epstein was in many respects a soul mate of John Lennon's, particularly in his rejection of conventional institutions. He had a disappointing career in school which included expulsion at the age of ten from Liverpool College. He wrote in his 1964 biography, *A Cellarful of Noise*, "I was ragged, nagged and bullied by boys and masters. My parents must have despaired many times."

Despite his failures in school, Brian developed an interest in art and the theatre and, at one point, aspired to be a dress designer. However, parental opposition and societal pressures finally led him into the family business, a department store in Walton, Liverpool.

Here he proved his abilities as a natural salesman and store designer. This first successful venture was rudely interrupted when he was drafted into military service. Here again, as in school, he proved to be a failure. "It was like prison," he said. "I did everything wrong."

He was discharged on medical grounds and returned to Liverpool to immerse himself even more deeply into the family business.

His fondness for the arts continued to develop and he began to concentrate his interests in the record department of the store.

Brian's aspirations to become an actor lured him away from Liverpool to the Royal Academy of Dramatic Arts for three terms.

But, disillusioned with actors and their social life, he was easily persuaded by his father to return to I. Epstein and Sons. This time he began a concerted effort to improve the record shop. He opened two new successful stores in the city center in Liverpool and one in White Chapel. His stores became famous for personalized service which included procuring obscure and difficult-to-obtain records.

Though his musical tastes were mainly classical, Brian started a pop top-twenty sales list. He also started reviewing new record releases in the Liverpool pop paper, the Mersey Beat.

With his business booming and his reputation well established, Brian began to feel restless, a timely feeling, it turned out, because a customer came into the shop on October 28, 1961, and requested a German disc called "My Bonnie." Though Epstein had never heard of the record or of the group the Beatles, he made a note of it and, as was his policy, began trying to track down the disc. The more he researched, the more curious he became about the Beatles. He found that they were a local group and had a large following of fans—including some of his employees—and that they played at the Cavern. Brian was naturally shy, so he asked The Mersey Beat to arrange admission for him to the club.

To his surprise he recognized the band as customers who frequented and loitered in his shop.

Brian was immediately intrigued by the intensity of the performance of the band and their rapport with the audience. He quickly decided that they had great potential. He said of his first exposure to them that "they were not very tidy and not very clean. They smoked as they played and they ate and talked and pretended to hit each other. They turned their backs on the audience and shouted at people and laughed at their private jokes. But there was quite clearly enormous excitement. They seemed to give off some sort of personal magnetism. I was fascinated by them."

He was particularly fascinated by the most raw and raucous member, John. Almost immediately, Brian offered to be their personal manager. John, speaking for all, immediately accepted. Said John, "He (Epstein) looked efficient and rich."

With financial help from his brother Clive, Brian started NEMS Enterprises to handle the Beatles. He then set about using his promotional abilities to increase their bookings and pay.

He insisted that the boys clean up their act. He sent them written instructions on his personal letterhead about how to dress and behave onstage. He began grooming them for the commercial market.

Cilla Black, then a hatcheck girl and singer who

was part of the local music scene, commented on their pre-Epstein image: "They had on these pink leather coats and those funny caps. The sound was *fab*. But the clothes were worse than ever . . . I thought only madmen would wear clothes like that."

Initially John balked at the idea of a transformation from his long cultivated "Teddy Boy" image. Epstein had them wear matching, tailored suits, some without collars. "Tell me if I look bloody awful," John begged his girlfriend.

Lennon said of Epstein's influence, ". . . he literally fuckin' cleaned us up and there were great fights between him and me over not wanting to dress up. In fact he and Paul had some kind of collusion to keep me straight because I kept spoilin' the image."

Performance techniques were tightened up. No more shouting, eating and throwing food were allowed on stage. Their sets were pared down to the tightest versions of their strongest material.

Brian set about obtaining a major record company contract. He had always had good relations with Decca records and decided to use this contact. He arranged for an audition in London on January 1, 1962.

They traveled through a blinding snowstorm on New Year's Eve, showed up at Decca with all their equipment, which they were told to remove, and waited their turn after the other auditioning bands. They felt slighted and nervous. They recorded demos of "Sheik of Araby," sung by George Harrison and "Red Sails in the Sunset" and "Like Dreamers Do," done by Paul McCartney.

Though the talent scout Mike Smith liked the

51

group, Brian was disappointed three months later when he was told that Decca wasn't interested. He recalled, ". . . a short plump man said to me: 'Not to mince words, Mr. Epstein, we don't like your boys' sound. Groups of four guitarists are on the way out.' I said, masking the cold disappointment which had spread over me, 'You must be out of your mind. These boys are going to explode. I am completely confident that one day they will be bigger than Elvis Presley.' "

At about the time of this early disappointment, John said, "I think Decca expected us to be all polished. We were just doing a demo. They should have seen our potential. I think a lot of halfwits were looking after it."

It was at this point that the group consciously began to exclude Pete Best by withholding the disappointing news. Best was more and more an outsider and learned of Decca's refusal weeks later, when one of the group accidently let it slip.

The Decca refusal was the beginning of a series of disappointments. Pye and EMI as well as smaller labels turned them down. The frustration mounted. "We did have a few little fights with Brian," John admitted.

Despite their impatience for results, the Beatles knew Brian was doing his best. He had been in the process of arranging a third Hamburg tour which took place in April of 1962. He had haggled for months with a club promoter, Manfred Weidlieder, for a contract which insured that the group would earn over four times what they had previously earned on other German trips. At Epstein's insistence, they flew to Germany. They were booked into the largest club in Hamburg, the

Star Club, a wild place where drunken sailors and bouncers clashed nightly. It was in places like the Star Club that the Beatles defined their sound, playing endless sets before rowdy audiences. They would do numbers like "Twist and Shout" with John screaming his way through the tune, backed by blazing guitars and pounding tom toms. "Twist and Shout" was their call-to-arms and a natural set opener. The crowds loved it. The scene was a far cry from earlier experiences from which the group returned exhausted and penniless.

They were reunited again with Astrid Kirchherr, still suffering over the death of her beloved Stu. They made every effort to console her and cheer her up.

Meanwhile, Brian was beginning to despair at landing a recording contract. His father, too, was pressuring him to spend less time on wild projects and more time in the family store. He decided to make one last-ditch effort—if he was not able to sell the Beatles this time, he would give up the project.

Hoping to make a more impressive presentation, he took the demo tapes to the HMV record center, a subsidiary of EMI in London, to transfer them to a record. The man who cut the disc was so impressed that he passed the tape along to music publisher Syd Coleman. Coleman was enthusiastic and wanted to take over the group's publishing. He also contacted a friend, George Martin, who produced comedy and jazz records for another EMI subsidiary, Parlophone. He knew Martin and Parlophone had been looking for new talent like skiffle and rock bands. George Martin listened and liked what he heard. He told Brian Epstein, "I believe you have something very good here." He agreed to a recording session. Brian, the happiest "Liverpudlian in London" wired the good news to the Beatles in Germany on June sixth:

CONGRATULATIONS BOYS
EMI REQUEST RECORDING
SESSION PLEASE REHEARSE
NEW MATERIAL

Exitedly the Beatles began to rework two Lennon/McCartney tunes, "P.S. I Love You" and "Love Me Do." Epstein flew to Hamburg and, after hearing the tunes, renegotiated their contract.

They returned to England to audition for Martin. Their play list included some of their original tunes, "P.S. I Love You," "Hello Little Girl" and "Love Me Do."

Martin personally liked the group. "I found them very attractive people," he recalls. "I liked being with them, which was funny, I suppose, as they were so insignificant and I was so significant. It shouldn't have really mattered to me whether they liked me or not, but I was pleased they seemed to. I discovered that John was a fan of Peter Sellers and his Goon Records I'd produced."

Martin also liked the sound, but did not give the Beatles any firm commitments. So the group returned to Liverpool once again unsure of their future.

Their popularity was reaching greater heights. They were named the number one group in Liverpool by a Mersey Beat poll. They played a triumphant welcome home party which jammed the Cavern, and sold out clubs and dance halls all over West Lancashire.

Then the big break came. In July, a recording

contract was negotiated with EMI. But there was one fly in the ointment. Pete Best had to go. His relationship with the group had continued to be strained.

According to Epstein, "George Martin had not been too happy about Pete Best's drumming, and the Beatles both in Hamburg and at home had decided that his beat was wrong for the music . . . though he was friendly with John, he was not liked by George and Paul."

Ironically, it fell to Brian, who got along better with Pete than the other group members, to break the unhappy news.

The replacement for Best was the Beatles' old friend from Hamburg, Ringo Starr. As well as his playing with Rory Storm and the Hurricanes, he had toured Butlin's Holiday Camps and U.S. Air Force bases.

Ringo was officially welcomed into the group by John, who told him, "You're in, Ringo. But the beard will have to go. You can keep your sides though."

Best had a huge following of loyal fans who were enraged when they heard he had been sacked from the group. Their old fans at the Cavern who already suspected that they had sold out after their transformation from leather boys to pop singers had their wildest paranoia confirmed. A furor erupted in Liverpool and controversy surrounded the city's most popular group and anyone connected with them.

Angry crowds gathered outside the Cavern chanting pro-Best and anti-Ringo slogans. George Harrison even sported a black eye earned while defending their new member. John looked back on the incident with some regret: "We were cowards when we sacked him. We made Brian do it. But if we'd told Pete to his face, that would have been much nastier than getting Brian to do it. It would probably have ended in a fight if we'd told him."

Brian remained undaunted despite the unpleasantness and controversy. He realized that to break the Beatles away from their Liverpool ties and reach a larger market, they would eventually disillusion some of their old fans.

Amidst the controversy, John and long-time girlfriend Cynthia Powell were married. Quiet, attractive Cynthia had found that she was pregnant with their first son Julian, and she was not sure how John would take the news. "I didn't know if John would want to get married," she said. "I didn't want to tie him down." Looking back on events she reflected, "I don't know exactly when John and I decided to get married. It just began to seem that we both decided on it privately and suddenly we were talking about what we were going to do after we were married, and then he just looked at me and said, 'Hey, we're getting married.'"

John told it a little differently. "I was a bit shocked when she told me, but I said, 'Yes, we'll have to get married. I didn't fight it." He went and told Mimi, who only groaned at the news. They were married at the Mount Pleasant Registry Office in Liverpool on August 23, 1962, and celebrated with a chicken dinner after the ceremony. John remembered the ceremony: "There was a drill going on all the time. I couldn't hear a word the bloke was saying."

Consistent with his lifetime desire to keep his personal life a secret from fans, John told no one outside of the group. "I thought it would be good-bye to the group, getting married, because everybody said it would be. We went mad keeping it a secret. None of us ever took any girls to the Cavern because we thought we would lose fans, which turned out to be a farce in the end. But I did feel embarrassed being married. Walking about, being married. It was like walking about with odd socks on, your fly open."

Cynthia, too, was wary of public identification with John, especially in view of the increasing number of hysterical girl fans. "It was bad enough John being chased everywhere. I didn't want that to happen to me."

On September 11, 1962, the Beatles cut their first record with George Martin. They picked the haunting "Love Me Do" with John as vocalist with "P.S. I Love You" for the flip side. Regarding the choice of material Martin recalls, " ' Love Me Do ' was the best of the bunch in the end. It was John's harmonica that gave it its appeal."

It was at these first sessions that Martin recognized John's ability. "John was the rebel, the Dylan of the group, and much more a word man than Paul. Paul learned about words from John."

The band was nervous, but Ringo as the newest member was really on the spot. Martin wasn't ready to risk precious studio time with an untried drummer, so he had a session drummer stand-in. As it turned out, they did a good number of takes, some of them with Ringo on drums, and the final choice had Ringo playing on "Love Me Do," but he played maracas on "P.S. I Love You."

While the group returned to Hamburg for extended club engagements, "Love Me Do" rose to number 17 on the pop charts.

Brian knew what was needed was a blockbuster hit to insure the group's upward pop mobility. Martin suggested that the group record the catchy "How Do You Do It," later recorded by the Beatles' Liverpool rivals, Gerry and the Pacemakers. Martin thought the song seemed to convey the clean-cut image the group was being groomed for, and it was bright and facile enough to please a pop audience. After cutting it as a demo the group decided against it. It was too much of a sacrifice of their artistic identity. Instead, they insisted on recording one of their own songs.

They chose to do something they would do again many times in subsequent years: taking a signature they'd already established and amplify it beyond its original effect. The musical and dramatic high point of "Love Me Do" was the harmonized "Plea-ea-ea-ease" at the end of each verse. They took that part and built another song around it, "Please, Please Me." Using the same elements, they created a more explosive version of "Love Me Do," including John's harmonica part, and built to the incredible chorus of "Please, please me, oh yeah, like I please you."

This record defined the Beatles as a totally unique group in British popular music. It was powerful and irresistable rock and roll, not just more vocal group music.

While the Beatles were touring as the opening act to Helen Shapiro, "Please, Please Me" hit number one and they started getting warmer receptions than the headliner.

The next step was to put out an album which

would show the Beatles in their most positive light. The album destined to be a rock and roll classic opens with the Lennon/McCartney composition "I Saw Her Standing There."

McCartney opens the song counting down the intro to a shout, punching it open with a driving bass pattern, singing in the gravelly hoarse tone he cultivated after years of listening to Little Richard. His vocal plays tautly against John's low harmony. The chorus climaxes like a skyrocket swooping through the arrangement.

The influence of Phil Spector's Motown "wall of sound" is noticeable in the song's dense rhythmic pattern and handclap punctuation. In this technique, the instruments are recorded and mixed in such a way that they are indistinguishable from each other and produce a monumental wash of sound.

The individual vocal styles of each member of the band became obvious on this album. Ringo sings the lead on a jumping number called "Boys" and John, belting out the lead in "Twist and Shout," transforms the rhythm and blues staple into a rock classic. John sings several other songs on the album, including the mournful "Anna," the wrenching "Baby It's You," and, of course, "Please, Please Me." It took sixteen hours to record the album and it stands out as an impressive achievement.

At almost the same time they completed their third single, "From Me to You." It was pretty much a reworking John's approach to the first songs. The song reached number one, mainly because of the pleasant melody and the commercially sentimental message, but it did not signal any new artistic developments for the group.

On August 23, 1963, they released "She Loves You," a single that would permanently establish their notoriety. It became the anthem of a generation trying to find its voice. It was an expansion of "Please, Please Me"'s most successful moments, developing the suggestive "O yeah" into an overwhelming chorus of "Yeah, yeah, yeah." It was a positive affirmation of humanity, an acceptance of life. The universal message—Yes.

"Yeah, yeah, yeah" became their trademark. Beatlemania was triggered by this refrain and those words explain their success more than any others. The Beatles appeared at a time when the world was experiencing great social stress. England had been shocked by the Profumo scandal, America by the Kennedy assassination. The time was ripe for a message of joy, simplicity and hope and the Beatles gave this to a generation facing a future filled with incomprehensible problems.

Beatlemania hit with such an impact that "She Loves You" hit half a million records before anyone had heard the single. The next single, "I Want to Hold Your Hand," had advance orders of a million copies.

On October 13, 1963, the Beatles first appeared on British national TV on a show called "Saturday Night at the London Palladium." More people watched it than had watched the Coronation Day Ceremonies—over fifteen million people. Outside the theatre throngs of fans caused an all-day furor. The media ate it up and the next day the papers were splashed with headlines and lead stories describing the mayhem resulting from the concert.

Epstein was shocked to see how quickly things had gotten out of hand. He had beautifully handled their astoundingly rapid six-month rise from provincial obscurity to national prominence. He had begun to manage other Liverpool acts like Cilla Black, Gerry and the Pacemakers and Billy J. Kramer, who had just recorded a hit with a Lennon/McCartney tune, "Do You Want to Know a Secret."

But the Beatles' quick and overwhelming success was something else. Epstein recalled, "What I worried about was all of us becoming overexposed. At first sight the endless discussion in the newspapers of the Beatles' habits, clothes and views was exciting. They liked it at first and so did I. It was good for business. But finally it became an anxiety. How much could they maintain public interest without rationing either personal appearances or newspaper coverage? By a stringent watch on their bookings and press contacts we just averted saturation point. But it was very close. Other artists have been destroyed by this very thing."

The Beatles handled their place in the spotlight perfectly. They were open, childlike and humorous. They set a flippant anti-establishment tone for the generation that listened to them by poking fun at institutions.

Their interviews were often a series of one-liners and non sequiturs as they put-on reporters, already confused and mystified by them.

When "She Loves You" prompted an unprecedented reaction in Sweden, the Beatles did a five day tour there. When they returned home, hordes of screaming fans turned Heathrow airport into a mob scene.

They were invited to play for the Queen herself at the prestigious Royal Variety performance. It was at this show that John coined his famous one-liner when he asked the audience to clap along to a song and then added, "Those of you in the cheap seats clap; the rest of you just rattle your jewelry."

Beatle memorabilia began inundating the market. The Beatles could be seen everywhere—on lunch boxes and pencil cases, bags, buttons, wallets and, of course, there were Beatle wigs.

Then came the hit that would take America by storm, "I Want to Hold Your Hand."

No provincial Liverpool band had ever before made it in England. The Beatles were a fluke. The possibility that they could make it in America, home of rock and roll, seemed slim. British pop music until this point was a pale reflection of the gutsy American teenage music. The biggest English pop stars, Cliff Richard and Tommy Steele, never had any success in America.

Beatlemania was first reported in the States as some kind of amusing social phenomenon—a tame English version of the teenage hysteria that surrounded pop stars like Elvis and Sinatra and often exploded into the rock and roll riots of the '50s.

Two singles, "Please, Please Me" and "She Loves You," had been released in America with little reaction, and a business trip to the States by Brian Epstein had no result.

"I Want to Hold Your Hand" is what did it. Its

simple melody and driving beat were like nothing else on the American airwaves. The Beatles were English and they had a funny name and long hair. They were interesting. They captured the imagination of America. In no time at all, the song sky-rocketed to number one. "She Loves You" was re-released and followed "I Want to Hold Your Hand" to the number one spot.

Epstein seized control at once, arranging for a few key bookings and two headline engagements on the Ed Sullivan Show. He also convinced Capitol Records to spend the awesome amount of $50,000 on advertising and promotion. This combined with the news-hungry press set the scene so that on February 9, 1964 when the Beatles arrived at Kennedy airport in New York, they were mobbed by a crowd of over 10,000 hysterical, screaming fans. They were rushed into their limos to the Plaza Hotel, which was also surrounded by thousands of cacaphonous teenagers who had been waiting patiently in the cold for hours to glimpse their heroes. The scene was to be repeated hundreds of times over all around the world during the next three years.

The Ed Sullivan debut is legendary. It was America's first close-up look at this phenomenon. Looking back on it now, you can remember how long their hair looked. You can remember trying to sort them out—which one was which. Parents sneered and said they all looked alike with those "mopheads."

The music had little to do with the event. George Harrison was sick and their performance was less than spectacular. It was the reaction of the audience to the sheer presence of those four boys from Liverpool that built the scene to mythic proportions.

The Ed Sullivan Show, that great American Sunday night institution of traditional family entertainment, was invaded by an alien force of youthful enthusiasm. The post-war baby boom had reached adolescence and was making itself heard. Decorum was smashed. Each announcement of the coming moment was greeted with squeals and frenzied screaming. Sullivan was outraged and threatened not to bring out the Beatles at all if the audience didn't quiet down. His stern schoolmaster tone contrasted violently with the joyful anticipation of the crowd. Somehow the upwardly mobile-first generation immigrant-World War II veteran ethic was violated by all this. But the tradition goes even further back to the American Puritan suspicion of letting go, of having too much fun. And while the rules violated were those of fashion—"Their hair is too long"—or social decorum, many of the older generation sensed a threat to the order of their life plan of working hard, saving money to better yourself and acquire better things in life. They were right. The lines were beginning to be drawn and before long the term "generation gap" would become part of the English language.

There was something about the wit and innocence of the band that so fit the spirit of the times. The press conference scene was repeated so many times with reporters asking straightforward dumb questions and the band responding with absurdities. Lennon, especially was noted for his non sequiturs and quick responses. "Genial anarchy"

*Beatles on the Ed Sullivan show. Screaming
from the audience almost wrecked the mikes.*

was what *Newsweek* called it.

The first few Beatle concerts are amazing in retrospect. The music, good as it was, had little to do with their live performances. The music was on the radio, everyday, everywhere. Everybody knew the words to the songs.

A Beatles concert was an event; the concerts were the first gatherings of the generation that would find itself at Woodstock six years later. To most of the large crowds in arenas like Washington's Coliseum or Forest Hills' tennis stadium, the Beatles were tiny figures in the center of a mass of humanity, jumping with excitement and energy and united in their enthusiasm for the band. As the group ran onto the stage, a deafening roar blew across the crowd like an enormous wind and sustained itself in varying degrees throughout the performance, dying down only at the end of each song and starting up again as soon as the crowd could identify the first few notes of the next song. The music was in the minds of the audience. They really couldn't hear anything except what was in their heads.

Only a small number of the audience could actually see the individual Beatles, but most could only identify them by their positions on stage and their physical gestures, which they knew from TV and the masses of printed matter about the band. It was all a very funny, absurd kind of ritual.

This was true for the band as well. They were often faced with ridiculous situations. Once in Washington they were placed on a stage in the center of the arena and had to switch their set-up every few numbers to face the opposite direction. They unceremoniously stepped over their am-

In the early days, John proved himself to be the most
literate and certainly most outspoken of the group.
His sarcastic brand of humor attracted attention in
both movie and TV realms and his books of witty
verse won him literary acclaim.

plifiers with Ringo in the worst position, having to turn his entire drum kit around, while the cymbals tottered and crashed onto the stage.

At the longest, their sets included eleven songs, starting off with "Roll Over Beethovan," "From Me to You," "I Saw Her Standing There," "This Boy," "All My Loving," "Love Me Do," "Please, Please Me," " 'Till There Was You," "She Loves You" and "I Want to Hold Your Hand." Overall, that's a pretty short show, but since the band realized that it was less a concert than an event, anyway, it worked out fine. The first few seconds of each song were the most important. But as soon as the screaming took over after the audience recognized the song, the band would just go on, virtually mimicking themselves since they, too, couldn't hear any of the music. They just stood there, clowning around, and playing something resembling the song, all the while being pelted by jelly beans and dodging the hysterical fans who tried to climb on stage.

The next three years—1964, 1965, and 1966— were a continuous whirlwind of daily one-stop engagements around the world. Without any question, the Beatles had become the most celebrated performers of the twentieth century—of all time. They played before more people in a shorter amount of time than anyone ever before. And still in the midst of this chaos, they made films and continued to write and record albums.

The filming for *A Hard Day's Night* began in March after the band had returned from America. Richard Lester directed the black and white film, which has become a classic of modern comedy.

The basic plot revolves around 36 hours in the life of the Beatles, and is structured as a virtually non-stop chase scene, opening with three of the Beatles being chased by hysterical fans to their London-bound train in Liverpool Station. Paul, with his fictional movie grandfather, played by Wilfred Brambell, sneaks onto the train in disguise. After a series of comic incidents and musical interludes reminiscent of the Marx Brothers, they arrive in London only to be chased again to their hotel. Grandfather serves as the plot thickener and manages to get Ringo into jail. The film resolves itself as the group, having just sprung Ringo, just makes it through the screaming hordes into the studio in time to film a TV special, which gives them the opportunity to finish off the film with a song.

The movie really was a case of art imitating life. There were moments during the filming when the paid extras—supposedly under the director's control to get hysterical on cue—could not be distinguished from the unpaid Beatle fans there to see their heroes.

But in real life, the problem of arriving late for a show was a constant during the band's tours, where the unexpected could always be counted on to happen. The sound quality was often poor at their venues, but one promoter had forgotten to run electricity to the stage. When the band arrived, they found no place to plug in their amplifiers.

After the craziness in Hamburg, the band was used to a frantic pace. But for virtually three years, their life must have seemed like an endless tape loop of hotels, airports, screaming kids, limosines, arenas and endless hassles with opportunists trying to shave a little piece from their success.

They worked incredibly well under pressure. In the breaks between tours they were in the studio. The sessions that produced the first two albums were tentative and even clumsy at times. But George Martin gave them direction and the band held its own, occasionally flashing brilliant. Most of the material were cover versions of American rhythm and blues records that the Beatles had played during their club dates.

Martin recalls their performances as pure adrenalin. "They really did try to work up a lather in the studio, which is awfully difficult to do under the clinical conditions of the studio. They learned very fast," he told *Rolling Stone's* Chris Hodenfield. "They knew nothing at all about recording to begin with. They got the techniques right off, very soon."

Rather than being exhausted by the grueling tours, the Beatles seemed to thrive on it. It was as if they were energized by the excitement surrounding them, and they continued to produce music that got better and better as the years went on. So much of the early material must have first seen light in hotel rooms or on airplane flights from city to city, with John coming up with a lyric or Paul pulling a melody from the air—a little collaboration and presto! Another Lennon/McCartney composition.

"Can't Buy Me Love," their first single released after their American debut, shows how well they worked under pressure. Lennon and McCartney wrote the song while on their way to Florida for

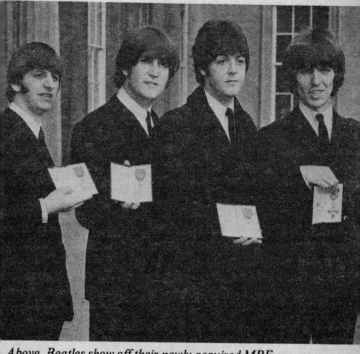

Above, Beatles show off their newly acquired MBE medals. John Lennon's father later accused his son of selling out to the establishment by accepting the award.

the second Ed Sullivan show as a send-up of their instant fame and wealth, and recorded it before they started the *Hard Day's Night* sessions. McCartney sings the lead vocal with Lennon doing the background harmony. Ringo beat out a backbeat behind them with his cymbals clattering against Lennon's acoustic rhythm guitar, and Harrison's lead guitar is double-tracked to add a crazed bit of subtlety. Without even working up a sweat, rock and roll was being pushed to its limits.

Then they started recording the tracks for *A Hard Day's Night*. "We wouldn't take more than a day on each track because they were busy doing concerts, doing the film. Titles had to be done very quickly," George Martin remarks.

It was the first Beatles album with only original material, and it was an indication of even greater things to come. Rockers like "A Hard Day's Night," "I Should Have Known Better," "I'll Cry Instead" and ballads like "And I Love Her" and "If I Fell" were much more sophisticated than their earlier songs.

The plot of *A Hard Day's Night* looked tame compared to their second American tour. This time the media and the local authorities were ready—or so they thought. As many as 10,000 fans greeted the band at each of the airports along the way, despite the fact that there were news blackouts concerning the date and time of their arrival. The Cow Palace in San Francisco was their first gig and the San Mateo County Sheriff's office had put together what they thought to be a clever security arrangement. The Beatles were ushered off their plane into a car and driven to an unused section of the airport where they were placed on a one=foot=high platform, surrounded by a six foot cage of fence so they could be protected while the fans could see them. "I guess they think we're four monkeys," quipped Lennon.

Hotels, scared off by the hoopla, cancelled their reservations and last-minute arrangements had to be made. The police in various cities started duping fans with decoys and re-routing procedures, but when the Beatles complained about this in a radio interview in Chicago, the police in Detroit, their next stop, responded by providing no protection at all. The band was nearly ripped apart by over-enthusiastic fans who jumped on them outside the Whittier Hotel. A lot of luck and a good deal of humor managed to get them through.

Two more albums and a series of blockbuster singles were recorded within the next year in an astounding display of productivity under pressure.

Outstanding were the two-sided hit of late 1964, "She's a Woman" and "I Feel Fine," which employed sustained feedback techniques for the first time in a hit single; and "Ticket to Ride" which featured a ringing electric guitar sonority in its theme anticipating the Byrds and influencing Southern California folk rock.

Help, their second film, was much less of an artistic success than *A Hard Day's Night*. A slick parody of the then popular spy genre, filmed in color and on location in the Bahamas and Austria, it lacked the sincerity and innocence of *A Hard Day's Night* and offered nothing in exchange. The music, however, was another story, and gave a strong indication of the direction that each of the Beatles was going in as individuals. Harrison contributed his first compositions to a Beatle album, "I Need You" and "You Like Me Too Much." In addition, his guitar playing was improving enormously. Some sitar music was used for the soundtrack, and before long, he was investigating Indian music seriously.

The niceties of the pop idiom had always bored Lennon and his sarcasm, cynicism and rawness provided an edge to the Beatles' music, tempering McCartney's tendency toward the saccharin. The tension between the two is what gave so much strength to their collaboration, combining the two extremes of Lennon's hard-rocking rebellion and McCartney's melodic appreciation of everyday life.

John's restlessness was sincere. Always on the lookout for new ideas and new ways of expressing them, he kept the Beatles in the vanguard of musical and cultural change throughout the 60's. One result of this openness was an interesting cross-cultural influence between the Beatles and Bob Dylan. Dylan, inspired by the Beatles, abandoned his solo acoustic folk music format, switched to electric guitar and formed a band. Lennon, upon hearing Dylan's phrasing, storytelling ability and penchant for social commentary, went in that direction himself. In addition, Lennon reportedly was turned on to pot for the first time by Dylan.

The seventh album, *Revolver,* showed the effects of various outside influences on the Beatles, and the personality of each member of the band became clearly focused for the first time.

McCartney, the balladeer, produced "Eleanor Rigby," a timeless song about alienation and

The critics were slightly less enthused about Help *than they were about* Hard Day's Night. *In all its daffy joyousness, though, it did manage to land very good reviews.*

loneliness. Harrison contributed three songs, "Taxman," "I Want to Tell You" and "Love You Too," which expanded his use of the sitar to a rhythm and lead role. "Yellow Submarine" provided a vocal lead for Ringo, laying the foundation for his later recording persona. It was Lennon who made the most far-reaching changes; influenced by drugs, he came up with the most unusual song on the album, a transcendental hallucination called "Tomorrow Never Knows," which opens with the line "Turn off your mind, relax and float downstream."

George Martin remembers that "John wanted his voice to sound like a Dalai Lama on the top of a hill. He wanted it very sort of atmospheric. We laid down the track with Ringo on drums and a tamboura drone, and I put John's voice through a Leslie speaker to make a weird noise. For the background we've got all these tape loops and I got tape machines from all over the building at EMI; in fact, we used sixteen."

Lennon was becoming as outspoken in his personal life as on his recordings. He made his most notorious statement in 1966, when, in an interview with Maureen Cleaves of the *London Evening Standard*, he remarked: "Christianity will go. It will vanish and shrink. I needn't argue about that. I'm right and I will be proved right. We're more popular than Jesus now. I don't know which will go first—rock and roll or Christianity. Jesus was all right but his disciples were thick and ordinary. It's them twisting it that ruins it for me."

The news reports all over the world proclaimed Lennon had declared the Beatles more popular than Jesus Christ. The reaction was pure outrage.

In Birmingham, Alabama, a local radio station sparked a nationwide protest declaring it would no longer play any Beatles on the station. Station manager Tommy Charles stated, "We just felt it was so absurd and sacrilegous that something ought to be done to show them they cannot get away with this sort of thing."

Thousands of somber-faced Beatles fans ritualistically participated in public burnings of Beatle records and effigy lynchings. The response was so overwhelming that Brian Epstein flew to New York to hold a press conference and attempt to lessen the impact of the controversy. Lennon did apologize for the remark, but the Vatican paper, *L'Osservatore Romano*, in accepting the apology, complimented Lennon's social perception by noting that the statement had provided Christians with "a well-placed kick where it was most needed." The British *Catholic Herald* actually went so far as to state that "if a worldwide opinion poll could be taken, we should probably find that John Lennon was speaking the bare truth." Lennon, in his insistence on not shrinking from controversy, pointed out a lack of spiritual values in today's world, and despite the knee-jerk reaction from some, the remarks did provoke thought. Rev. Richard Pritchard of the Westminster Presbyterian Church in Madison, Wisconsin, blamed the very people who expressed outrage at Lennon's remarks for their validity. "Those people should take a look at their own standards and values. There is much validity in what Lennon said. To many people today, the golf course is also more popular than Jesus Christ."

Lennon's capacity for inspiring social dialogue

was just beginning. He was to become increasingly radicalized in his stand against war and for consciousness expansion. The controversy was to continue.

The future of the Beatles was to be in the recording studio, not on stage. "No one eventually enjoyed touring," Ringo explained. "It was wrecking our playing. Eventually I just used to play the off beat, instead of a constant beat. I couldn't hear myself half the time, even on the amps, with all the noise."

1966 marked a turning point for the Beatles. Like their fans they were maturing. The time for the screaming teenyboppers had passed. Largely at Lennon's insistence, they retired from the stage and began a new approach to songwriting and album craft. Before the Beatles, long playing records were only a small part of the recording industry, which was centered around the 45 rpm single. Usually, an album was just a collection of incidental tracks surrounding the latest hit which was usually used as the album's title.

It was the Beatles who first produced albums in which each track was important. A new standard in quality and cohesiveness was approached in albums like *Beatles '65, Rubber Soul* and *Revolver*. Lennon, however, wanted to carry the idea even further, to an album that was a completely unified concept.

By a strange coincidence, the main theme of the album was reflected in the social phenomenon occuring in San Francisco, the last city in which the Beatles ever played. Mind expansion drugs, mysticism and a joyful affirmation of life had been taken up by the city's youth, carrying the anti-establishment tradition of the beatniks one step further. People called them hippies. The Beatles, who had been evolving along the same lines, were inspirational to them.

After months of concentrated work, the album was released. *Sgt. Pepper's Lonely Hearts Club Band* literally tried to change the world. The Beatles had reached their greatest efficiency in recording. It was the crowning achievement of the recording process, both technically and aesthetically up until that point, a sweeping redefinition of the limits of recorded music. Lennon demanded the impossible from George Martin, and because he was so insistent and because Martin was ingenious enough to find the sounds that Lennon had in his head, they were able to achieve on a 4-track recording a production that rivals today's 16- and 24-track technology.

What Lennon was hoping for was an evocation of his generation's image of the quality of life. It was a manifesto of the generation that was determined to make up its own mind about the world. Suddenly, in the summer of 1967, young people all over the world united behind the mystery and imagination of this record. They rejected the rampant materialism that had been held up to them as their goal in life and were determined to seek a new meaning for existence, in a quest for brotherhood, universal peace and cosmic consciousness—terms which today have deteriorated into meaningless cliches. The central image of the music was transcendental spiritual awakening through the glorification of the LSD experience. Lennon pointed out in "Lucy in the Sky with Diamonds" that it was all there for the asking.

The band had grown up with this generation. But the traditional teenage themes of romantic love and social economic frustrations were being replaced. The audience was on the verge of adulthood and the Beatles began to write songs about things like infinity, the loss of self in a cataclysmic religious experience and the need to open everyone's heart to universal peace.

These are questions that have concerned thoughtful people for all time; it was a herculean task to attempt to work out these theories through two sides of a long-playing record. Many other musicians attempted to deal with these subjects with embarrassing results. But the Beatles managed to keep the project simple enough to work as a conventional record, but complex enough to completely revolutionize recording techniques.

The Beatles' confidence in their recording and the universality of their songwriting were, of course, important factors—but the album could not have been effected without the production genius of George Martin. He approached their material as an outsider, unaffected by the emotional excesses, pretense or paranoia which inevitably result from an artistic endeavor of this kind.

He helped the band express their ideas with clarity in the most accessible and appealing way possible, using traditional recording conventions. The string arrangements on Harrison's "Within You Without You" and Lennon/McCartney's "A Day in the Life" are similar to the hundreds of muzak string arrangements that Martin had produced over the years. But Martin used them deftly and was able to augment an Indian raga and simulate an LSD rush.

The album cover, a funeral piece, was meant to indicate that a change had come over the group. Without a doubt the message was clear. The madcap fabulous four Beatles promoted all over the world by Brian Epstein were dead. Epstein was upset about the cover and suggested that the albums be packaged in brown paper, an amusing irony in retrospect to the *Two Virgins* cover uproar.

Drugs are clearly the theme. Ringo as Billy Shears opens with an anthem like "I Get High With A Little Help From My Friends," followed by "Lucy in the Sky with Diamonds," "Fixing A Hole" and "For the Benefit of Mr. Kite," hallucinatory fillers. The optimistic, life-renewing character of the album is embodied in "Getting Better," and "She's Leaving Home" is the central song with the Beatles for the first time addressing themselves to the generation gap, spelling out one of the reasons for teenage rebellion ("fun is the one thing that money can't buy"). The song is sentimental, but so accurate that it works.

Martin, looking back on the sessions, remarked to *Rolling Stone* magazine, "It certainly affected the music but it didn't affect the record production because I was producing . . . I saw the music growing, but I rather saw it like one of Salvador Dali's paintings. I didn't think the reason for it was drugs. I thought it was because they wanted to go into an impressionistic way. I wasn't looking for any sinister reason for it. I hotly denied it when people put two and two together and made five, like "Lucy in the Sky with Diamonds" meaning LSD . . . One of the greatest problems, always with John and Paul, particularly John, was trying to find out what was going on in his mind. He wasn't particularly articulate in saying what he wanted. Of course when you're dealing with a dreamlike substance, it's very difficult to be articulate. My main job was trying to get out of him what he was trying to get. It came together more in the mix than it did in gradual growth. I saw the way things could be done, for example, cutting things together in the track. We had a lot of barnyard animals on "Good Morning." There was a chicken sound in one of these, and a guitar noise from another thing, the guitar actually turned into a chicken."

In 1967, the "Summer of Love," when hundreds of thousands of young people across the globe took acid messiah Timothy Leary's advice to "Turn on, tune in and drop out." *Sgt. Pepper's Lonely Heart Club Band* became the theme. Once again the Beatles had struck the right chord in the generation. Rock and roll was growing up.

Late in the summer of 1967, *Sgt. Pepper* was riding a massive crest of popularity. As *Sgt. Pepper* was becoming the anthem of the global psychedelic awakening, the Beatles were on their way to confer with the Maharishi Mahesh Yogi for instruction in the methods of Transcendental Meditation. They were all in Bangor in North Wales when they heard the shocking report. On August 27, 1967, Brian Epstein, at age 32, had died from an overdose of the barbiturate Carbitol.

Sgt. Pepper may have been a self-conscious attempt by the Beatles to cut themselves off from their past, but the death of manager Brian Epstein such a short time after its release gives the album a chilling portent. When the band left the road and live performances to concentrate solely on studio work, Epstein's responsibilities were almost non-existent, but his death signalled the point at which the Beatles really began to break up. Fortunately, in the breakup phase, the band was still able to produce some great music.

Idealism and self-absorption had been a very effective working environment for the Beatles while Epstein was their manager, but without him acting as their trusted agent, they were unable to screen out the realities of the outside world. Brian had protected them fanatically. Without him to orchestrate their activities and buffer them with savvy business decisions, the Beatles' idealism became their most vulnerable point.

Sgt. Pepper had created a new vitality in the band, especially in the heady glow of its strong recording sessions. During that time, while Brian was still alive, the Beatles had decided to get into their own movie production rather than going the route of a third straight conventional feature. The group had renewed their commitment to each other and their partnership by forming a new corporation. This creation—Apple—was formed for the purpose of maintaining artistic freedom over their creative decisions. In a bid to change the system from the inside, they tried to set up a totally idealistic corporate entity. They considered the option of creating several non-profit foundations which would also provide for tax deductions. They had many plans for the Apple corporate umbrella. In what they perceived as a 'consciousness raised' attitude, the Beatles treated money cavalierly and thought of this as the chance to do some good with the wealth they had earned.

In the vacuum that appeared after Epstein's death, McCartney tried to take up the mantle of leadership. He was most interested in delineating the band's tangled relationship with Epstein's business organization, NEMS, so that the band could push through their film project to completion. *Magical Mystery Tour* had been stalled for most of 1967 mainly because the group and some of the staff couldn't decide whether it was a worthwhile project.

Neil Aspinall, their road manager who evolved into a general manager, talked about the chaos and indecision that surrounded the project even in its production phase. "We went out to make a film and nobody had the vaguest idea of what it was all about. There were these incredible scenes dashing about the west of England with a busload of actors. We didn't know any of them and they were forever complaining that they wouldn't share a room with somebody or other. We went all the way to Brighton, yet when we got there, we ended up filming two cripples on the beach. What we should have been filming, if anything, was all the confusion, because that was the real mystery tour. We should have filmed John Lennon ripping the damn signs off the bus to stop people following us. We should have filmed the carloads of reporters trailing around after us, or the chaotic traffic jams we caused whenever the bus got stuck. The problem was that with Brian dead, there was nobody to organize anything. Before he died, you'd ask for twenty cars and fifteen hotel room and it would all be taken care of."

The project was wreathed in chaos but that was appropriate to the era. The Merry Pranksters were involved in their own chronicling of a cross-continental hallucinogenic bus tour and the "go with the flow" sensibility ruled. McCartney's insistence pushed the film to completion and it was released on British television during the Christmas holidays. The film turned out to be an interesting reprise of the drug-related themes and acid imagery that had energized *Sgt. Pepper*. What the film suffered from more than anything was the lack of overview and mediation that George Martin had provided on the *Sgt. Pepper* project. The Beatles directed *Magical Mystery Tour* without any real professional assistance, and it showed. It was an amateur production that turned out to be incomprehensible to anyone who was not tuned-in to the abundant drug references. The biggest mistake was that the film was first released on television, at that time, a black and white medium. The film's visual beauty, which might have carried it for those who could not understand, was lost without color. Had the film been held off from the mass medium, it may have been appreciated for what it was; but the group decided in a fit of hubris to release it with fanfare as a special .Beatle production. Perhaps they did it to try and exorcise their feelings that the Beatles couldn't do it without Epstein.

Their first project after the demise of Epstein was obviously an out and out calamity. *Magical Mystery Tour* was raked over the coals by the

British press. Like sharks crazed with the smell of blood, the press made a lot of red-hot copy out of the Beatles' failure to produce in their first major project after the death of Epstein.

George Harrison had the most to do with getting the rest of the group acquainted with Eastern philosophy and spiritual technique. It was his interest that led them to Bangor on the eve of Brian Epstein's death. In 1968, George was in Bombay, India, working on recording the soundtrack of a film called *Wonderwall*. A short time later George and the rest of the Beatles returned to India. They went to undergo a complete course in the Maharishi's Transcendental Meditation techniques. All of them arrived at the Maharishi's Academy at Rishikesh with open minds and apparently high expectations. Their visit had been widely ballyhooed in the press and it was made to seem important that the Beatles had taken time off from being the Beatles to make the journey of study. Once at the Academy, however, things got off on the wrong foot almost immediately. The meditation training was always of short duration and was sporadically scheduled. It seemed that the Maharishi was going Hollywood. He seemed far more interested in the publicity that he was soaking up than he was in relating to the Beatles themselves.

Any hopes that the Maharishi might have had of having input into the Beatles' direction after the void left by Epstein's death dissolved rapidly in India. Ringo was the first one to fly the coop. He took off after two weeks, leaving with the wry but telling comment that he didn't care for the food. McCartney was on Ringo's heels soon after that. Lennon stuck it out with George, but when the

86

Maharishi began to get too overt about his obvious fascination with the charms of Mia Farrow, John, too, had reached the end of his rope. John was so incensed with the whole fiasco that the guru had fobbed off on them that he took the time to tell the Maharishi that he thought he was a shyster.

Upon returning to England the group found that their financial world was in a complete uproar. Clive Epstein, Brian's brother, and Robert Stigwood, Brian's administrative assistant were the people who seemed to be the likely successors to the power structure that Brian had left behind. Stigwood, who had helped Brian assemble talent, took all that he had learned from Brian plus some of the talent that Brian had developed and left NEMS to start his own management company. Clive was not the flamboyant type that Brian was and felt uncomfortable with most of the NEMS interests, including the Beatles, and decided that he wanted to concentrate on NEMS' television interests. Clive arranged it so that the Beatles would be left to their own devices as far as NEMS was concerned. This situation seemed to please the band and they began at once to put most of their creative talents and financial resources into the fledgling Apple Corps.

They saw Apple as the ideal umbrella organization under which they could sponsor any number of creative projects. The Beatles as individuals had been pursuing ideas completely outside of the group context ever since the release of *Sgt. Pepper*. They perceived Apple as an institution that would provide them with the finances to carry out any of their ideas or fantasies either individually or collectively. The bank of creative projects in various stages would be supported by collective spiritual base.

That idea was probably one of the central themes to their concept of the alternative corporate ideal that they were trying to create. They remembered that when they had taken the road of success out of Liverpool, many of the bands from the area had been able to follow the same success route. The Beatles probably assumed that a similar situation might occur from the new route that they were taking.

They started out by trying to incorporate some of their old friends from the Liverpool days into important staff positions at Apple. They then set aside two million dollars for Beatles projects, but, more importantly, a good deal of that money was earmarked for developing the creative ideas of other artists that needed support.

The Beatles were completely and idealistically sold on the merit of the project. They went so far as to come to America to promote the idea in the press. John was especially active in this area and he and Paul had a number of interviews in New York in only a few days. The most important of these interviews was the *Tonight* show. Unfortunately, it was during one of Carson's frequent vacations and the guest host that conducted the interview was Joe Garagiola, who couldn't seem to get a grasp on the subject. Garagiola distorted the interview process to such an extent that most of the people that witnessed the interview were left with the idea that the Beatles were saying that they were interested in giving money away. The audience couldn't have taken what John and the others were trying to get across too seriously.

The failure to get their idea across properly to the American press and public foreshadowed the practical problems that occurred in reality when they tried to set up their business utopia. The attitude at the top of the Apple Corp. (The Beatles) was one of "hands off, everything will happen naturally, stay loose."

That attitude certainly filtered down through the ranks, and it was all too apparent at Apple headquarters. Richard DeLillo, who spent a great deal of time in the Apple office, was prompted to write a diary of his stay there; he titled the journal, *The Longest Cocktail Party*. The Apple staff had set up what they thought would be the perfect counter-culture answer to the stuffy atmosphere of big-time corporate headquarters. In the beginning, Apple always made sure that there was enough food and drink for the people who worked there and for people who had business to transact at the offices. That situation got out of hand when the office became a hangout for all kinds of freeloaders. Most of them had some kind of scatterbrained scam to run down, most with an artistic wrapping: poems, screenplays, books or strange inventions. Derek Taylor, the public relations man, had his office constantly filled with journalists who were hanging out sucking up the free stuff. These diverse crews began to mix regularly each day and the drinking would begin earlier with each day. It seems as if the scene eventually attained a semblance of some modern day beggars' banquet.

The business ventures that they tried to launch belied what was happening back at the office. For a long period of time the Beatles had thought about investing money in a chain of retail stores. With the advent of Apple it seemed an even more attractive idea. The reasoning was that the retail business would generate money that could be funnelled back into worthwhile projects that were conceived by artists with no money. It was a praiseworthy concept. The idea took form in the Apple clothing boutique on Baker Street in London. It took about 250,000 dollars to set up the shop and it was supposed to be the apex of the type of boutique that was springing up all over during 1967.

The first problem with the boutique happened right at the start. During the television production of "All You Need Is Love," the Beatles had gotten involved with, and to some extent supported, a group of psychedelic artist/designers called The Fool—they designed the costumes for the TV production. The Beatles hired them to design the boutique. Seeing that Apple was serious about a trusting stance and easy business standards, The Fool immediately took advantage of and reportedly cheated the Beatles out of a large sum of money. When the store opened, the employees were quick to recognize the same situation and attitudes. They began to pocket sums of money at any opportunity—and apparently, the opportunities weren't rare. Before the close of the summer of 1969, the Apple boutique was closed. They went out with a gesture typical of their business dealings at that point. The last $35,000 worth of merchandise was given away.

John Lennon hired a man who called himself "Magic Alex," Alexis Mardis in reality. Mardis was supposed to energize Apple's electronics division. What Apple actually funded for Alex was a laboratory in which he reportedly spent tens of thousands of dollars to create inventions like a stroboscoping electric apple, some kind of radio phonograph and a highly complex box loaded with expensive electronics which apparently did nothing.

The biggest disappointment in the Apple empire was the records division. Apple released two singles that were immensely popular right at the start: "Hey Jude" and Mary Hopkins' "Those Were the Days." It seemed from that point that Apple was destined to make a great deal of money. Yet the rest of the projects that Apple tried to undertake were failures. The person who was charged with discovering and signing musicians to the label was Peter Asher (formerly of Peter and Gordon). Asher actually did a fine job. He came up with two very talented songwriters, James Taylor and Jackie Lomax. Apple wasn't able to spring either of them. The album that Taylor made with Apple sold only a few thousand copies and it wasn't long before he split from the company. Jackie Lomax created a fine album which inexplicably didn't make much of a splash. Eventually, he also left Apple but his career never really took off. On the other hand, James Taylor became a highly successful pop performer within a short time of his departure from the Apple fold.

Apple's record division did make money on the Beatle albums. The first one was popularly known as the "white album," because there were no markings on the jacket other than the low relief title, *The Beatles*, in white on white. The white album sold at a greater volume than any of their previous recordings.

The musicianship of the recording is good and the production of the actual instrumental sound is the most far-ranging combination that they ever put down. It varies from the mean, rough distortion of "Yer Blues" to a lilting, cheery and melodic "I Will."

Sgt. Pepper was a very positive statement, replete with the upbeat "We can change the world." Psychedelic consciousness, *Magical Mystery Tour* and *Yellow Submarine* amplified that side of the vision. The white album could be interpreted as the other side of that coin. The record contains a number of songs that were conceived and at least partially worked out in India when the horror and futility of Epstein's death had had time to sink in and become an accepted fact. The group head was also affected by the exposure of the Maharishi, a man they had invested with some trust and respect, as a charlatan. The white album is the bad trip; it is laced with bizarre violence-filled visions of despair and betrayal.

McCartney seems to try and maintain the upbeat feeling with the clever parody, "Back in the U.S.S.R.," the carefree "Ob-La-Di, Ob-La-Da" and the simple love songs "I Will" and "Martha My Dear." But in "Blackbird" the plaintive line "take these broken wings and learn to fly . . ." gives an indication of the depth of sorrow that was surrounding the group at that time.

Starr is even moved to strike a somber note with his notable contribution "Don't Pass Me By," and George Harrison's mood seems to be one of bitterness and resignation typified by the biting

In August of 1967, three Beatles joined about 15,000 other Londoners at a Kashmiri yoga's lecture on transcendental meditation and took part in a five minute mass meditation which followed. Afterwards, The Beatles joined the lecturer, the Maharishi Mahesh Yogi, backstage for an hour-long private session.

"Piggy" and poignant "While My Guitar Gently Weeps."

John Lennon, on the other hand, is completely outspoken in the depth of his rage and disillusionment. His effort to make the bullshit and pettiness fade away by trying to ignore it and by trying to set a better example for people was thrown in his face. He lashed straight out at the Mahrishi in "Everybody's Got Something to Hide Except Me and My Monkey," and his guitar in this song sounds mean, brutal and full of reflected distortion. He follows that with another swipe at the guru, "Sexy Sadie." "Yer Blues" is the capper; Lennon pours out his bitterness, frustration and isolation screaming about his own death and loss.

It's not surprising that the record contains the hellish nightmare song "Helter Skelter," which Charles Manson used as the anthem of his coterie that loosed a spate of brutally deranged murders and mutiliations.

A few years after its release Lennon offered this perspective on the white album, as a signal that the band was falling apart: "The Beatles white album. Listen all you experts, listen, none of you can hear. Every track is an individual track. There isn't any Beatle music on it. I just say listen to the white album. I don't know what the album before that was; was it *Pepper*? *Pepper* was the one and only, you know. I don't think Paul ever liked the white album really. It was John and the Band, Paul and the Band, George and the Band, like that."

George Martin has an interesting comment on the production of the white album. "They came through a bad time about then. I was puzzled about the white album, why they wanted to make a double album with *all* the material. They had about thirty-six songs, they wanted to get into a studio and record them all and they shouldn't have. . . . I don't think they were particularly artistic. They were sort of businesslike, and 'Let's get these songs recorded.' And I think it came out that way."

This lack of communication among the group was telling, especially concerning something as important as the relase of a new album. The Beatles as a group of friends and as individuals had vested Apple with hope and idealism. But business had a way of bringing out certain characteristics in a very harsh light.

McCartney was the member of the group who took the business aspects of Apple most seriously. It appears that he wanted to really take the company in hand and mold it into a workable form. But he didn't have the knowledge to do a project of that magnitude properly. Yet inevitably, he must have begun to play a role of corporate leader. This was complicated by the fact that he was having to work on the band's artistic efforts at the same time. Most likely, he carried some of his play-acting into the studio and the people who had known him that long didn't buy it. McCartney began to get on the bad side of Ringo and George.

McCartney, who is an excellent drummer in his own right, was frequently very specific in his playing instructions to Ringo and apparently Ringo had some feelings of insecurity. "It can get you down, not being creative," Ringo commented on his feelings at that time. "You know people are thinking you're not the creative one . . . I do sometimes feel out of it, sitting there on the drums, only playing what they tell me to play. Often when drummers of groups say to me, 'that was great, that bit,' I know the others have usually told me what to do, though I've got the credit." At one point during the production of the white album Ringo walked into Paul's office and stated that he was leaving the band.

George Martin remembers that there was a growing clash between McCartney and Harrison, too. "He didn't like Paul's bossiness. George wanted to be in front with the other two and I'm afraid he didn't get a great deal of encouragement from me either, which was unfortunate for him."

Lennon remained noncommital about the pettiness of the recording sessions, but he was not so quiet about what was happening at Apple where Paul was playing the Boss. Lennon also knew then that Apple was losing a lot of money rather than generating wealth for redistribution. "In the early days," Lennon remembered, "we vaguely had an ideal about British music and that if we could break through and make it to America, others could break through after us. We got trapped in the ideal of Apple and were swamped with the bums and freaks that everyone else had been turning down for years. When Apple was at Wigmore St. I used to see everyone who came in, and I used to spend the whole day turning away complete rotters. If Apple was going to be what the ideal for it was, I would have to spend the rest of my life sifting through other people's songs and stuff. We had to get back to being musicians and being ourselves."

Ringo voiced similar feelings. "Since Brian died," he said, "we've sort of been torn apart. We have to look after ourselves and do everything Brian did, even though sometimes we thought Brian did nothing. You know you get like that, when everything is going smoothly you think, 'he's not doing anything,' but he really was. He had his office that did everything we have to do now. I mean all I want to do is play. If I wanted to be a businessman I would never have taken up drums.''

They were all so confused and alienated by the world and all their possibilities that they couldn't talk to each other anymore. They had years of shared experience and humor that carried them along for some time after they stopped really speaking to each other. But in the end the humor probably turned to extreme sarcasm and as a device to puncture and wound. Blow-ups that had previously been a vented pressure became more serious. There was also a certain amount of strain that came from each of them getting more interested in people outside the group.

During the hassles that marked the production of the white album, Lennon apparently took no part in the confrontations. One of the main reasons was that he had begun his deep absorption in Yoko Ono. Yoko was with John throughout the bickering.

George Martin sees this as a critical element to the confrontations that would develop later. ''The disruption rally came with the women anyway. When you have very close personal relationships between two men, and one of them goes off and gets a girl, then there's a divergence. I don't think that Paul minded Yoko, Yoko's fine, nothing wrong with Yoko, except that she was always there. When she wasn't well she had a bed in the studio, and the other boys got fed up with that. I think that was the beginning of it. And almost in self-defense Paul got Linda. There you go.

"People talk about the break-up of the group as though it was a tragedy and so on, which is nonsense. They don't say it's amazing how long they lasted together. What other group has lasted as successfully as they have? And as amicably as they? For nearly a decade, it really is pretty remarkable. It's amazing to me, human nature being what it is, that they didn't break up earlier under the strain of superstardom. They were living in a golden prison all the time, and living with each other and not growing into individual lives. Now they're living individual lives and enjoying it. Good luck to them."

That's an essential observation that gets to the heart of the Beatle myth. The Beatles were symbolically adolescents, and all were part of the pack. Women didn't fit into that sophomoric idea. Lennon's marriage with his Liverpool girlfriend, Cynthia Powell, was hushed up in 1962. Harrison's marriage to Patti Boyd and Ringo's wedding to Maureen Cox were similarly kept out of the public eye, even though fan magazines played up the fact that three of the four were no longer eligible bachelors.

Those three early marriages had all fit nicely into the mold of most British middle class unions and none of them upset any of the group's internal chemistry. Apparently, the women were content to sit in the background and they tried hard not to be noticed. There was a notable example of this lack of public consciousness as to whom the Beatle's wives really were when the group took the Bangor train to see the Maharishi. Cynthia Powell could not make it through the security at the rail station. The police would not believe that she was Lennon's wife. She was left behind when the train departed.

One cannot imagine that kind of thing happening to Yoko Ono. Yoko was very visible in John's company. The two of them undertook creative projects together, like Yoko's conceptual art shows and her films like *Smile*, which was a 90-minute movie of John smiling. Their most famous project was the *Two Virgins* record album, whose cover sports John and Yoko in the nude. This was decidedly not at all in keeping with the standard Beatle image.

In the context of the group, John's involvement with Yoko was a highly political act. John's subsequent pot bust and immigration struggles in the U.S. only intensified the negative press they were getting surrounding their campaign for peace, which was most newsworthy in the "Bed-Ins" that John and Yoko created (after John's un-Beatle-like divorce from Cynthia) on their Amsterdam honeymoon. It is possible that George Martin was correct when he suggested that McCartney's marriage to Linda Eastman, later in the month than John and Yoko's, was a defensive reaction.

John felt the reaction to his relationship with Yoko was negative and it seemed to bewilder him. "I still feel part of Apple and the Beatles and there's no animosity," he said at the time. "But they tend to ignore Yoko and me. For instance, Kenny Everett recently made a promotional record for Apple which was played at the big yearly EMI meeting. It plugged James Taylor, the Ivies and so on, but it didn't mention the things Yoko and I have been doing. And I think what we're doing is a lot more important than James Taylor . . . Apple seems to be scared of us.''

Their growing individuality was not the only thing that was threatening the stability of the Lennon and McCartney relationship. One of the big factors was the huge rat's nest that their financial entanglements had become. A great deal of pressure was placed on the group to straighten out the finances. Their loose, trusting arrangement deteriorated when they had to determine who got how much.

The root of the problem was the death of Brian Epstein. Brian's death left both the Beatles and NEMS without a manager. NEMS controlled about twenty-five percent of the Beatles royalties from records; this percentage came from the original royalty agreements with Epstein. The fact that the Beatles were no longer on the road and touring made the royalties a very important piece of the pie, perhaps the most important slice.

When Clive Epstein made plans to sell NEMS to Leonard Richenberg's firm, Triumph Investment Trust, the Beatles suddenly panicked. One of the things that the group had so emphatically worked to avoid was threatening to break in on them again: a strange group of men in grey flannel was about to buy a piece of them. When Epstein received a share it did not matter that much because he had been with the group from the beginning. He had worked hard with them and had been in some sense responsible for getting them started. But the Beatles who were very aware of the generation gap were angry that a group of bankers could take the piece that Brian Epstein had sweated for and earned, just by shuffling some money around and buying up his company now that he was dead.

The Beatles had the idea to try and buy Brian's company themselves, shutting out the bankers that way. Had they been able to present a concerted effort and legal front they probably would have had a good chance of winning their bid. But the tensions within the group, especially between Paul and John, precluded that.

The group had been seeking a manager for some time. They were chastened by the continuing disaster at Apple and realized that they needed someone with experience to come in and clean up the mess. Unfortunately, the problem of straightening out the Apple empire was so great that all the financial wizards that the group approached took one look at the situation and declined to even try to sort it out.

Linda Eastman's father, Lee Eastman, was an established show business lawyer. McCartney eventually sought him out and asked advice on handling the NEMS/Triumph affair. Lee suggested that his son John should handle the situation. He also wanted to have John Eastman take over the management of the group.

John Eastman put together a counter-plan for the Beatles to buy NEMS before Triumph could take it over. The offer he put together was for a million pounds. Eastman had gotten a promise from EMI chairman Joseph Lockwood to advance the Beatles one million pounds against their future royalties.

Lennon at the same time was casting about on

his own for a manager. He had admitted in public that Apple was ailing and made what amounted to a general appeal for help. "The problem is that two years ago our accountants made us sign over eighty percent of our royalties to Apple," Lennon said in his statement. "All the money comes into this little building and it never gets out. If I could get me money out of the company, I'd split away and start doing my own projects independently. I'd have much more freedom and we'd all be happier."

Allen Klein, a New York business man, read Lennon's comments and they went off like a sky rocket in his mind. He placed a call from New York to London as soon as possible. Lennon took the call and Klein convinced Lennon that a face-to-face meeting was in order. Klein quickly flew to London.

Klein had already managed the Rolling Stones and had reportedly boasted that he was destined at some point to manage the Beatles as well.

When Klein and Lennon met, Lennon was immediately won over by the brash New York lawyer. In the first place, Klein was intimately familiar with the Beatles music and their careers; John Eastman, on the other hand, seemed not so familiar with what the Beatles had accomplished.

John was also impressed that Klein, like Lennon himself, had worked his way up to the top from relative poverty—and, he had done that even though he was an orphan, a note which must have struck a responsive chord in Lennon due to his own fatherless childhood. He was also taken with Klein's irreverence and his stance of thumbing his nose in the face of stodgy upper class authority.

Apparently the biggest reason for Lennon's acceptance of Klein was that Klein convinced Lennon that he would make it financially possible for Lennon to pursue his own projects. But even more appealing was the promise that there would be enough money to finance a number of Yoko's ideas for art shows and films in addition to Lennon's own albums. Klein also convinced Lennon that with him running the show, he could even make those films turn over a profit.

The day after that meeting, Lennon walked into Apple headquarters and announced, "I don't give a bugger what anybody else wants but I'm having Allen Klein for me."

When Klein had learned about Eastman's plan to buy NEMS, he arranged a meeting with the Beatles and got an agreement that the deal would be held in abeyance until Klein was able to complete a three week investigation into the total financial picture of the Beatles. Lennon, Starr and Harrison agreed, but McCartney angrily and abruptly left the meeting.

At this point it seems that the Beatles had, in effect, split. McCartney was set on having his in-laws manage the group's future, but Lennon had convinced the others that retaining Klein would be in their best interests. McCartney wouldn't give ground.

Triumph took advantage of the chaotic state the group was in and they got hold of NEMS before the Beatles knew what hit them. Their situation continued to deteriorate. Klein felt that the issue was not worrisome at that moment because he had convinced himself that he would be able to void the sale on a technicality. NEMS supposedly owed the Beatles a great deal of money from the days when the band was still touring.

Clive Epstein felt that the reason that the Beatles lost NEMS was the manner in which John Eastman had negotiated. "Eastman spent a week negotiating for NEMS," said Epstein, "on the basis of the loan that Lockwood was prepared to make the Beatles but he loaded the offer with so many conditions and warranties that he ended up talking himself out of the deal. In my opinion he was a little too young to be negotiating at that level." Klein tried to go on the offensive against Triumph by making a bid to annul the deal because of the owed royalties question. Richenberg didn't back down and he knew he held a valid contract. He ordered an investigation of Klein's personal and business finances, and a tax discrepancy was discovered in Klein's involvement with one of his former record companies, Cameo-Parkway.

Klein had this to say about the Cameo-Parkway charges: "There has been an enormous amount of back-biting. You won't find one client of mine who says I wasn't honest. As far as Cameo-Parkway is concerned, they were delighted by the stock exchange because of their poor earnings records before I bought them out; they were bankrupt. I was never accused of any wrong-doing."

Klein had been rocked a little, but Richenberg hadn't knocked him out. He kept on the offensive; he had the Beatles go straight to EMI to try and get some results. The Beatles ordered EMI to pay all royalties straight to Apple instead of NEMS. EMI had over a million pounds in hand and was ready to deliver. After that sally EMI decided to hold payment until the matter was entirely settled in court.

Klein had forced a stalemate that only the courts could sort out. It was a brilliant strategy, considering the nature of the disputed assets. There were income-producing assets and also human assets—the band itself. If the whole operation was at a standstill, a whole lot of money was going to be lost. Richenberg had been outflanked. After he tried a number of times to meet with the band members individually and failed repeatedly, he finally agreed to sit down and negotiate with Klein and the Beatles as a group.

Klein's reputation as a tough negotiator proved justified. He worked out a deal in which Richenberg dropped Triumph's claim on the royalties from one-quarter to one-twentieth. In return, Triumph got shares in several Beatle-related companies.

Throughout this humbug, Klein was renegotiating the Beatles recording contract at EMI. He eventually worked out a deal for the group which effectively doubled their royalty rates. This deal shocked the record industry. Klein had established his credibility for good with John, Ringo and George.

McCartney was, however, adamant in his refusal to accept Klein in any manner or form. He refused all of Klein's advances and it seems that many of the employees at Apple were sympathetic to Paul's stance. Klein had moved through the Apple offices like Sherman through Atlanta and he fired many people in a very short time.

Secretary Chris O'Dell described Klein's "new broom" very effectively. "He just moved in and started firing people," she said. "It took him a year to do it, but in that time he got rid of everybody he could possibly clear out, either by taking their work away, so that there was nothing for them to do, or by making their jobs so uncomfortable they felt obliged to quit . . . He didn't like people who were close to the Beatles. He was worried they would go back and report to them."

Lennon's reply to this kind of talk was direct. "It takes a new broom and a lot of people will have to go. It needs streamlining. It doesn't need to make vast profits, but if it carries on like this all of us will be broke in six months." Ringo seemed to have similar feelings, but he didn't express them as strongly as Lennon. "All we're trying to do now is get a hold of ourselves. Just pull in on ourselves because we're owned five percent here and five percent there. There's always someone who has his finger in. We're trying to take all those fingers out of the pie and have it just for ourselves."

People at the time were wagging their heads and commenting that it was a shame that the Beatles, and especially Lennon, had gotten involved with such a high pressure business type. The new manager seemed to be the antithesis to everything that the group had tried so hard to establish in alternative Apple.

Lennon answered those criticisms apparently without seeing much validity in them. "We got Allen in because we needed someone to run it." Lennon said. "What he did was fire a few people and give them letters saying they weren't fired so that they could get jobs elsewhere. We found out we couldn't run it. Not one of us could run a company, that's the mistake we made.

"We wanted to be the Ford Foundation," he continued, "and we couldn't do it. We didn't know how to and didn't have the money. When I made the statement that Apple was broke and losing money, it was true. Everyone was taking a free fucking ride on us. The only way for us to help other people and do these things is to get as much money as possible and then give it away. But we were giving it away before we had it. Now it's just about organized. The first thing we have to do is watch after our own records, and anything else will come after that."

Klein added his bleak assessment to the picture of the mess at Apple. "They were totally locked up and losing money, spending far more than they were making. Their money all went into Apple, but Apple wasn't really theirs. We had the books audited and Apple lost one million dollars in the first year, if you exclude Beatle earnings. I closed down Apple Electronics because it was doing nothing. Apple publishing had four employees, but nobody was doing anything.

"They set up companies but there were no rights properly given to any of these companies. Peter Asher never even signed James Taylor to Apple Publishing, and even so, we are under threat of suit from CBS, which claims that it owns publishing on most of the songs on the James Taylor LP."

The thing that emerged most clearly from all these suits and disputes was that the Beatles had been dismantled. They were only an idea.

The last big battle was over control of the Beatles' own music publishing company, Northern Songs. A company, ATV, headed by British financier Lew Grade, was moving in to take possession. Once again the Beatles were not legally organized nor were they spiritually unified enough to withstand the onslaught. They made what turned out to be a half-hearted bid to gain total control of the Northern Songs company. Between them Lennon and McCartney owned or controlled thirty-one percent of the stock in the company. But they had to stand together to make any kind of case. Apparently, McCartney still could not force himself to take part in a deal that Klein was part of, so the opportunity hung fire for a time. When it disappeared, and the Beatles had lost control of their own publishing company.

Klein ended up selling their shares in Northern Songs for ten million dollars. Had the two Beatles been able to get together, they could have gotten control of the company.

As all this legal wrangling was going on the Beatles had been trying to complete a film which they had decided to base around recording sessions for what would be their next album, *Let It Be*.

Phil Spector produced and released the album. John had nothing but praise for the work that Spector did on the project. "Phil Spector came in and listened to every take," said Lennon. "He changed the takes originally used. He listened to about one thousand million miles of tape, none of which had been marked or catalogued. Which is why the Beatles couldn't face the album, because there was too much shit and nobody was interested enough to pull it together. And Phil pulled it together, remixed it, added a string or two here and there. I couldn't be bothered because it was such a tough one making it. We were really miserable then. Spector has redone the whole thing and it's beautiful.''

George Martin has his own memories of how tough laying down *Let It Be* was. "*Let It Be* was the worst time of all, really disruptive. Basically because they were going through an anti-production thing. John said during *Let It Be*, 'I don't want any production gimmicks on this. I want it to be an honest album. I don't want any overdubbing of voices, got to be live. I don't want any editing. If we're going to do it and make a mistake that's hard luck. It's going to be honest.'

"But it got to the point where we would do a take and he would say, 'How was it, George?' I'd say, 'Well, it was pretty good but it wasn't perfect.' And he'd say, 'Was it better than the other one?' And I'd say. 'It was a little bit better than take 46, but not quite as good as take 53, and the back drums were not quite as loud as they were in 69.' It just became ludicrous. You're trying to get the perfect one live, it's ridiculous. And the album that I made of *Let It Be*, originally, was built on that premise that he insisted on. I was very shocked later on when he took it to Phil Spector and Phil overdubbed heavenly choirs and lush strings and harps and things, and John overdubbed the voice and did all the things he said he shouldn't in the first place.''

The most interesting thing in watching the film portion of the *Let It Be* project was getting to see how the group functioned in the studio. The film records all of the tedious steps in getting tuned and re-doing songs until it all fits together. Also there is the opportunity to hear some songs in the rough that finally appear on their final album, *Abbey Road*.

But the film is finally most interesting when seen as a visual record of the band breaking apart. Paul spends the most time in front of the camera and seems to take charge of the project—and that seems to ultimately cast him in the culprit's role. John is a counterpoint to the ubiquitous Yoko. He seems very removed, offering thin mocking smiles that seem to indicate that he knows what the camera's eye is pointing out. The only time he appears to be truly involved is when he dances with Yoko in one scene.

So the film instead becomes a document about Paul and how the others tolerate his foibles. This tolerance is lost in the parts of the film where Paul upbraids George. After a run-through of "The Two of Us," Paul criticizes George's guitar work. Paul begins to lecture the band as a whole after "For You Blue" and at one point actually turns away from them to let the audience look at him while he is "laying down the law." This is not long after a scene in which Paul is trying to convince George that this film won't be contrived like the other Beatle movies.

As the film unreels, Paul is acting out, John is fading out and George and Ringo are hanging out, with each other. George and Ringo seem to be trying to demonstrate comfort and support for each other throughout the increasingly strained proceedings. George sings "I Me Mine" while playing an acoustic guitar. The intent of the song seems clearly to take a shot at Paul for holding out his vote from the rest of the band in their legal processes; Ringo stands by George, showing his approval. Later, when Ringo is singing "Octopus's Garden," George sits close by and offers the same support for Ringo.

The part of the film where the band gets out on the roof of the Apple building to play for the passersby is legendary. It is the closing sequence of the film—and the last Beatles show that approximates an actual concert.

The music grows more powerful as the segment continues. People down in the streets below begin to stop and listen as "Get Back" heats up and finishes strong. People climbing up onto adjacent rooftops to see what's happening. "Don't Let Me Down" snakes down into the streets as traffic slows down and the police arrive to try and restore order before things really get out of hand. The band flies into "I Got A Feeling" and they move right onto a scorching version of "One After 909." Down below, the streets are completely choked and drivers get out of their cars to listen. The cops can't take it and decide to get to the bottom of things, so they start up for the roof. John and George are flying together. They whip into a climax with "I Dig A Pony" as George goes crazy on lead guitar.

The police make it up to the roof to be met by a reprise of "Get Back." The cops walk over and pull George's plug. But Paul and Ringo keep playing. George plugs in again and as the song winds down the police leave. The band finishes with a flourish, and Lennon says goodbye: "Thank you very much. I hope we passed the audition." It was the end.

The band actually got together one more time in

111

the studio, for *Abbey Road*. Lennon apparently had little interest in the project, especially the heavily-produced second side. He contributed "Come Together" and "I Want You (She's So Heavy)" to the first side. The band was indeed broken at that time, but no one outside of the organization knew it.

When the news of the breakup was finally made public, John seemed bitter and a bit shaken. In a caustic statement he summed it all up. "I'm telling you," said John, "that's what's going on. It's John, George and Ringo as individuals. We're not even communicating with or making plans about Paul. We're just reacting to everything he does. It's a simple fact that he can't have his way so he's causing chaos. I don't care what you think of Klein. Call Klein something else. Call him Epstein for now and just consider the fact that three of us chose Epstein. Paul was the same with Brian in the beginning, if you must know. He used to sulk and God knows what. Wouldn't turn up for the dates or bookings. It's always been the same, only now it's bigger because we're all bigger. It's the same old game.

"You know it's like this, when we read all this shit in the paper, Yoko and I were laughing, because the cartoon is this: four guys on a stage with a spotlight on them; second picture, three guys on stage breezing out of the spotlight; third picture, one guy standing there, shouting, 'I'm leaving.' We were all out of it."

JOHN
AND
YOKO

JOHN LENNON MET YOKO ONO IN LONDON IN 1966. At that point he was well into his period of drug experimentation, mind expansion and avant-garde consciousness. He was searching for new means of expression for both himself and the Beatles, and in Yoko he found an influence that would push him past the conceptual limits he had been working within up until that time.

Yoko was born in Tokyo in 1933, the daughter of a successful banker father and a socialite mother. After a fashionable schooling in Tokyo she was evacuated to the countryside during U. S. air raids in 1944. The family moved to New York in 1952 and Yoko enrolled in Sarah Lawrence College, where she studied for three years before dropping out to become part of the burgeoning New York avant-garde art scene.

At her New York loft Yoko Ono cultivated a salon atmosphere which saw many famous artists of the time call on her. "I was living on Amsterdam Avenue and I needed a loft in which to do my work," she later explained. Finally I found one and I gave my own concerts and art shows because no producer would think of giving them. My loft was a workplace that famous people happened to come to because it was an interesting place to visit. I was very poor and certainly not a young lady who gathered the famous about me in order to call attention to myself. I was very shy in those days and I could not even express my work properly. I created a painting to be stepped on and many artists, including Jasper Johns, Marcel Duchamps and Robert Rauschenberg stepped on it and didn't even know it was a painting. I went to a party with a crutch and acted as if one of my legs hurt. Everyone was so attentive to me but for all the wrong reasons. I didn't tell anyone that this was a crutch event and so they didn't know how to respond in the way I wanted them to. I needed to make instructions for people then because I was too shy to tell them myself.''

Yoko presented a series of shows at her loft-gallery while she was married to Japanese keyboardist Tochi Ichiyonagi, and some of the ideas she presented were well received. Her reputation grew to the point where she began to present conceptual works outside of her loft as well. "In 1964,'' she recalls, "in Judson Hall in New York City, I created an event called "Dawn Piece'' which was to go on until dawn. I asked everyone to shout the first word that came into their minds. The audience shouted their favorite motto or "mommy,'' "daddy,'' "I hate you,'' etc., and they went on and on. They were able to free themselves of all their aggravations. And it made beautiful music. Once I turned the lights off and instructed my audience to touch the first part of the body they could of the person next to them and just go on touching and rubbing it. Everybody giggled but believed that touch was very important.''

Yoko divorced Ichiyonagi and married Antony Cox, a filmmaker who fathered her first child, a daughter named Kyoko. She and Cox moved to London where Yoko stepped up her conceptual performances and began to work in films as well. Yoko's outlandish art raised plenty of eyebrows in the staid London art world, but many people were also intrigued and enthusiastic about her work.

A film called *Bottoms* was released and created some controversy because of its content. It was a series of images of backsides, reputedly British backsides, 365 of them in quick succession. Yoko described how she got the idea for *Bottoms* several years later. "I was in my house in Japan," she said. "A maid was scrubbing the floor and her bottom was sticking up. Then afterwards I saw a film—a corny film about cowboys—and a cowboy had his back to the screen and he was talking to another guy and a girl and his shoulders occupied about two thirds of the screen. I thought this was an interesting composition and I liked it. I thought that a film in which an object covers the whole screen and prohibits the filming of a background might be interesting. The audience would look at the screen and not be able to identify the object because there would be no background. Perhaps they'd think it was just a dark screen. The screen would move and they would not be able to tell if it was a flat surface or a surface with dimension. It could all be subtle and beautiful.''

Bottoms created an impact that earned Yoko a reputation in the underground London art world.

Her famous bag performance, in which she placed herself inside a black bag in public, also stirred up controversy, and her 1966 London show had created enough of a local buzz to interest John Lennon. Lennon recalls his initial reaction to Yoko's art. "There was another piece which decided me for or against the artist, a ladder which led to a painting which was hung on the ceiling. It looked like a blank canvas with a chain and a spyglass on the end of it. This was near the door when you went in. I climbed the ladder. You look through the spyglass and in tiny little letters it says, "Yes."

"So it was positive. I felt relieved. It's a great relief when you get up the ladder and you look through the spyglass and it doesn't say 'no' or 'fuck you' or something, it said 'yes.' "

Lennon was impressed by Yoko's thought process immediately. Then he met the artist that created this piece, and it was love at first sight. "That's when we locked eyes," said Lennon, "and she got it and I got it and, as they say in all the interviews we do, the rest is history."

At this point Lennon was still married to Cynthia, but he had changed completely since meeting his first wife and their relationship was no longer satisfying. But Yoko's influence on John pulled him even further away from the pop sensibility he'd carved with the Beatles. Lennon began to pull the conceptual limits of the band even farther away from what they thought the basis of their commercial strength was, and both Lennon and Yoko were resented for this.

"I sort of went to bed with this guy that I

liked," Yoko later explained, "and suddenly the next morning I see these three in-laws standing there.

"When I met John he was a typical male chauvinist," she went on. "He had been in an all-male group and he had come from a background where the men were all important. They were always having man-to-man talks and going to the pub together. Women were usually kept in the background, serving tea, keeping out of the men's talk. John never expected to meet a woman who would talk back, who would expect to share everything on an equal basis. But, you see, John is very quick to adapt to new situations. He comprehends things quickly and he understood that I was right. All the men and all the women around him were yes-men and he was getting tired of it and he was lonely. So from the beginning he did not want me to be another yes-man."

For Lennon, Yoko was the intellectual stimulation he had been looking for. "An artist is not usually respected in his own village," he pointed out, "so he has to go to the next town. It's a bit of that really. I think it's also a bit like Dylan Thomas and Brendan Behan, who were writers and both died of drink. Artists always die of drugs, drink and all that. Like Jimi Hendrix and Janis Joplin—it's just that they're so misunderstood and tortured that they kill themselves. I refuse to do that. I've found the way out. It's great. It's amazing that we think so alike coming from different ends of the earth. She's come from a very upper-class scene, going to school with the Prince and all that, and I'm from . . . wherever. It just shows that color, class and creed don't come in the way of communication. You don't even have to speak the same language."

Lennon's first post-Beatles project was an effort to present Yoko's musical ideas by producing her first record album, called *Two Virgins*. Lennon felt he was producing a thoughtful work of art, and he decided to release the record with a cover that showed a photograph of Yoko and himself naked. The other Beatles, their financial interests, and many members of the U. S. record industry were incensed by what they considered a pornographic move by Lennon. When initial copies from the British pressing were shipped into the U. S. they were immediately impounded by U. S. customs officials. Even when a compromise was agreed on that the record would be covered in brown paper wrapping, many distributors to U. S. record stores refused to carry the product.

When asked later if he expected the outraged reaction to *Two Virgins*, Lennon admitted that it had occurred to him. "Yeah, well I expected some noise about it. But I didn't expect as much as we got. I'm sure Yoko didn't expect it. I'd always wanted to produce Yoko, before we were lovers."

Lennon went on to explain that producing Yoko seemed to be the natural first step after leaving the Beatles. "It all started with the producing kick the Beatles got into. Paul was producing Mary Hopkins, George had Jackie Lomax so I decided to produce a record with Yoko. I was in India meditating on the Yoko album and how to present it. One day I just suddenly thought the best way was to have Yoko naked on the cover. I wrote and told her and I got some static on the other end. She wasn't too keen."

Lennon, as it turned out, had to talk Yoko into the idea. "Finally I had her persuaded. I came back to England and by natural turn of events I wound up being naked in the picture too. It was all a bit strange. When we were taking the picture I got a funny feeling when I looked down at me cock. Hello, I thought, we're on.

"When I got the pictures back, I was mildly shocked. You know, I was only mildly shocked, but I thought that if I'm surprised by it, what will others think? Then I looked again and I thought it was great having the *Financial Times* on the floor and everything. I'm pleased we did it. For all reasons, I'm glad about it. I wanted people to be shocked. It was all worth it just for the howl that went up. It really blew their minds like right-wing fascists."

The other Beatles were far from pleased. "I got long lectures from Paul about it at first. 'Is there any need for this,' he said. 'What are you doing,' said George. It took me five months to persuade them that it was right. That's why it took so long coming out. Now I'm planning to resell it. I'm going to promote it with a line saying 'It's still just a record despite all the crap that went on.' I wish more people had sat down and listened to it."

In retrospect Lennon was philosophical about the whole thing, though. "But the thing cleared the air a bit though," he reasoned. "That's why I'm glad. Anything that's headed toward the truth, the people try to trip it up. Their first reaction is to kill it, stop it from escaping. It is really showing them a mirror, showing them they're all ugly. But the album wasn't ugly, it was just a point of view."

Two Virgins was a decided break from Lennon's Beatles career, but it was not technically a post-Beatle project since it was released in the same month as the famous *White Album*. It did, however, provide a convenient marking place for the beginning of Lennon's post-Beatle career, as well as the beginning of the political troubles he would encounter. Shortly before the release of *Two Virgins*, Lennon and Ono were busted for possession of marijuana in London, a conviction which would come back to haunt them later when they tried to establish residency in the U.S.

Two Virgins was only the first step in a campaign by Lennon and Ono to use their celebrity status to promote world peace. While Lennon's first wife, Cynthia, was suing for divorce and using Yoko's relationship with John as part of the proof, it was announced that Yoko was pregnant with John's child. She later suffered a miscarriage.

In the summer of 1968 Lennon's artistic activities both with and without Yoko thrived. Lennon worked up some of his writings along with Victor Spinetti into a dramatic adaption for the British National Theatre. Then Yoko released another of her experimental films, *Film No. 5* which consisted of ninety minutes of John Lennon smiling.

"Last year," Yoko explained, "I said I'd like to make a smile film which included a smiling face snap of every single human being in the world. But that had obvious technical difficulties and it was very likely that the plan would have remained as one of my beautiful never-nevers.

"This year, I started off thinking of making films that were meant to be shown in 100 years time, i.e., taking different city views, hoping that most of the buildings in them would be demolished by the time the film was released; shooting an ordinary woman with her full gear—knowing that in 100 years' time, she'd look extraordinary, etc., etc. It's to apply the process of making vintage wine to filmmaking. This, in practice, would mean that as a filmmaker, you don't really have to make a film anymore but just put your name (that is, if you so wish) on any film and store it. Storing would then become the main endeavor of a film-maker. But then, the idea started to get too conceptual. That's the trouble with all my strawberries. They tend to evaporate and I find myself lying on the floor doing nothing.

"One afternoon, John and I went out in the garden and shot *Film No. 5*, the smile film, and *Two Virgins*. They were done in the spirit of home movies. In both films, we were mainly concerned about the vibrations the films send out—the kind that was between us. But, with *Film No. 5*, a lot of planning, working and talking out things had preceded the afternoon. For instance, I had thought of making *Film No. 5* into *Dr. Zhivago* and let it go on for four hours with an intermission and all that, but later decided to stick to a more commercial length of about an hour; 8mm copies of the film are also available for people who'd like to have the film on their wall as a light-portrait. Also, we'll store some copies for the next century.

"They say that in the corner of the world there is a man who sits and spends his life in sending good vibrations to the world, and when a star twinkles, we are only catching the twinkle that was sent 1,000 light years ago, etc.

"Imagine a painting that smiles just once in a

billion years. John's ghostly smile in *Film No 5* might just communicate in a hundred years' time, or maybe, the way things are rolling, it may communicate much earlier than that. I think all the doors are just ready to open now. One light knock should do. It's just that there are still a minority group in the world who are afraid of the doorless world to come. They're just not sure how they can cope with it. But most of us know that doors are just figments of our imagination. The good thing is though, that law of nature that once you know, you can never unknow things, so the doors are going to disappear pretty rapidly, I think.

"Some critic recently commented on us, John and I, as being lollipop artists who are preoccupied with blowing soap-bubbles forever. I thought that was beautiful. There's a lot you can do with blowing soap-bubbles. Maybe the future U.S.A. should decide their presidency by having a soap-bubble contest. Blowing soap-bubbles could be used as a form of swearing. Some day the whole world can make it its occupation to blow soap-bubbles.

"There wasn't any point in just making love, secretly and everything," Yoko offered. "We had to make a film which had the same vibrations as making love. A smile for everyone. That's us."

The two artists mounted a sculpture exhibit called "John by Yoko—Yoko by John" outside the Coventry Cathedral in England. The work is a pair of acorns planted in pots which were subsequently buried in the ground. People were to sit next to the pots and feel the acorns grow.

Lennon also put together a "For Yoko" show at the Robert Fraser Gallery. Tagged balloons saying, "You are here," and bearing the gallery address hung in the gallery by day and were released each night. "You are here" was also written on a white canvas in a white room in the gallery's basement, and the slogan is also printed on white buttons distributed at the show.

In March of 1969 John and Yoko announced their marriage in Gibraltar and dedicated a week of their honeymoon to a bed-in for peace at the Amsterdam Hilton. The U.S. was heavily involved in the Viet Nam war at the time and that involvement had become a major political issue, with many young people in America opposed to the war. Lennon took his stand for world peace earnestly, but most of the press looked on the bed-in as a grandstand move for publicity. The British press in particular attacked Lennon severely for the move, calling John and Yoko "utter fools."

Lennon later explained the bed-in as part of his idea, inspired largely by Yoko, to turn their public life into a work of conceptual art itself.

"When we got together," Lennon explained, "Yoko and I decided that whatever we did was gonna get in the papers, whatever people like us do would get in the papers. So we decided to utilize the space we would occupy anyway by getting married with a commercial for peace and also a theatrical event. The theatrical event we came up with which utilized the least energy with the maximum effect was to work from bed and what we virtually had was a seven-day press conference in bed. The press for the first day fought at the door to get in because they thought there was something sexy going on and they found two people talking about peace. Reporters always have five minutes with you or ten minutes with you. We let them ask anything as long as they wanted for seven days. And all the time we just kept plugging peace so the story became 'John and Yoko do bed-in for peace.' We were just promoting peace like you promote any product. They promote war: 'Join the Marines.' We were promoting peace.

"The naked album cover was less general than that, that was one of the first things we did. We felt like two virgins; that's what the album was called because we were in love, just met, and we were trying to make something. We thought to show everything. People are always looking at people like me, trying to see some secret, what do they do, do they go to the bathroom? Do they eat? We just said 'Here.' That was in 1968 and all hell broke loose but now people are going around naked all over the place, right? We were just ahead of our time."

The next step of this conceptual advertisement for peace came with a London press conference for which a major announcement was promised. The British press, which had fed off Beatles controversy for years at this point and sensationalized every detail they could get their hands on, moved in for the kill, asking hostile questions of the beleagered couple until the announcement was to be made. Lennon produced several packages which he held aloft for the reporters' inspection, then took one of the envelopes and opened it, revealing its contents to be a simple pair of acorns.

"These are our next move for peace," he noted. "Yoko and I plan to send one of these envelopes containing two acorns to the head of state of every

John and Yoko's Ascot mansion, above. Right, the newlyweds show off their marriage certificates. . .

John and Yoko in Toronto performing live for the first time together. An album came from the concert that included a blood-curdling version of John's powerful song, Cold Turkey. . . .

After the wedding at the stop over in Paris, John and Yoko set out for honeymoon in Amsterdam where they spent a week in bed trying to bring themselves and the world some peace. . .

country in the world. We want them to plant them for peace."

"And if they want us to," Yoko continued, "we would go to the countries and plant them ourselves."

This was far from the major statement the press had come looking for. They were looking for something juicy and ended up feeling that John and Yoko had tried to put something over on them. Inevitably, someone asked if the Lennon acorn pitch was a practical joke. "We are not laughing at you any more than you are laughing at us," Lennon replied. "It was just our protest against violence. Everyone has their bags, and this is ours. The way we look at it is this. In Paris, the Viet Nam peace talks have got about as far as sorting out the shape of the table they are going to sit around.

"Those talks have been going on for months. In one week of our honeymoon, we achieved a lot more. What? A little old lady from Wigan or Hull wrote to the *Daily Mirror* asking if they could put Yoko and myself on the front page more often. She said she hadn't laughed so much for ages. That's great, that's what we want. I mean, it's a funny world when two people going to bed on their honeymoon can make the front pages in all the papers for a week."

During the press conference someone asked Lennon if he was tired after his week-long bed-in for peace. "Mentally we are both still very alert," John replied. "But physically we are exhausted. In fact, we're going to bed for a week to recover."

This may have sounded like a good joke, but Lennon was in fact serious, because he and Yoko already had another week-long bed-in planned. Their design was to have it in New York, but U.S. officials did not take kindly to the notion. Lennon's visa allowing him entrance into the States was revoked as he was classified as an undesirable alien. That drug bust he and Yoko had been involved in turned out to be the reason for Lennon's official censure.

Upon learning that they were denied entrance to the U.S., Lennon and Ono figured the closest second would be Canada, so they chose that country, which was well known as a haven for U.S. draft resisters, to make their next pitch. They set up in a hotel room at the Queen Elizabeth in Montreal, inviting reporters in to talk from 10 A.M. to 10 P.M. for seven days. "The press is like a post box," Lennon explained. "They can reach the people—all the people—who are wandering around the streets."

Yoko made a few statements for peace as well. "We worked for three months thinking out the most functional approach to boosting peace before we got married, and spent our honeymoon talking to the press in bed in Amsterdam. For us, it was the only way. We can't go out in Trafalgar Square and join in because it would create a riot. We can't lead a parade or a march because of all the autograph hunters."

"We're all responsible for war," reasoned Lennon. "We all must do something, no matter what—by growing our hair long, standing on one leg, talking to the press, having bed-ins—to change the attitudes. The people must be aware that it's up to them."

In the suite at the Queen Elizabeth, John and

Yoko sat up in bed, holding hands contentedly, surrounded by a bed of white and pink carnations, cameras, tape machines and an autographed copy of Jacqueline Susann's *The Love Machine*. "The whole effect of our bed-ins has made people talk about peace. We're trying to interest young people into doing something for peace. But it must be done by non-violent means—otherwise there can only be chaos. We're saying to the young people—and they have always been the hippest ones—we're telling them to get the message across to the squares. A lot of young people have been ignoring the squares when they should be helping them. The whole scene has become too serious and intellectual."

When asked why he wasn't trying to talk directly with the world political leaders, Lennon replied, "Talk about what? It doesn't happen like that. In the U.S. the Government is too busy talking about how to keep me out. If I'm a joke, as they say, and not important, why don't they just let me in?"

Elaborating on the bed-in strategy, Lennon continued "Bed-ins are something that everybody can do and they're so simple. We're willing to be the world's clowns to make people realize it. If everybody stayed in bed for a week, there'd be no more killing. Right now we want to stir everybody, the whole world. Leaders can't exist without a following. We hope we can get the people to do something about the leaders."

Lennon explained that his movement for world peace could be construed as anti-nationalism. "I guess I'm a bit of an anti-nationalist. But I fancy myself as a bit of an Irishman. I think anti-nationalism will have to come if we want peace.

Beatle John returned his MBE back to Queen Elizabeth in November of 1969 to protest England's involvement in the Nigeria-Biafra conflict. He signed his protest "With Love."

We're really scared to go to the U.S. because people have become so violent, even our sort of people. Violence begets violence. We want to avoid it. But once we do get into the States, and can do our bed-ins in Washington and New York, I think we'll start to have some effect. I think it will take five to ten years to change things. Yoko thinks five; I'm for ten. But we can't do it alone, we must have everybody's help."

At one point during his Canada stay a reporter reminded Lennon of the furor caused by his statement about Jesus Christ. "I think I said that the Beatles have more influence on young people than Jesus Christ," he speculated. "Yes, I still think it. Kids are influenced more by us than Jesus. Christ, some ministers even stood up and agreed with it. It was another piece of truth that the fascist Christians picked on. I'm all for Christ, I'm very big on Christ. I've always fancied him. He was right.

"As he said in his book, you'll get knocked if you follow my ways. He was so right about that. We got knocked. But I'm all for him. I'm always saying his name, I use it in songs, and I talk about him."

One song in particular Lennon wrote about Christ was an account of the difficulties he and Yoko encountered in their peace promotion, "The Ballad of John and Yoko." It was a fairly journalistic account of each step of their drive for peace. In the stirring chorus of the song Lennon sympathizes with Christ, who he says knows it ain't easy. Then Lennon goes on to say that the way things look, he feels like they're going to crucify him too.

"The Ballad Of John and Yoko" as well as later

Lennon solo tracks like "Cold Turkey," "Give Peace a Chance," and "Instant Karma" were released under the name of the Plastic Ono Band, an idea which Yoko came up with when Lennon was trying to figure out what name to give his post-Beatle projects.

Later, when asked how she came up with the concept, Yoko explained, "I had a concept for a band that would never exist—a band made of transparent boxes with tape recorders and record players in their stomachs. It was admittedly a cynical attitude about bands, saying that a tape recorder and a record player could do just as well. But it led me to the idea of a conceptual group, an imaginary band without actual people in it. I conceived of the idea of a group that didn't have a set number of members, a group that could accomodate anyone who wanted to play with it. Everybody in the audience and everybody who wanted to play would all be a part of the band. John made a beautiful sculpture piece for me in which we glued transparent boxes with hands to a little stand. We actually made a few transparent stands and we were going to send them all over the world and let people play any music they wanted to. And that became my band. John gave it the name, Plastic Ono Band.

"Every time we record, it comes to life," she continued. "But we don't have a fixed number of members. Anyone who happens to be in the room can join. Sometimes, people who do not even play an instrument get up with us. They shout! They scream! It's marvelous."

The second John Lennon-Yoko Ono album, *Unfinished Music No. 2 Life With the Lions*, was a good indication of what Yoko was describing. The album was really a conceptual art work broken up into two ideas. Side One, entitled "Cambridge 1969," was a side long piece recorded live at Lady Mitchell Hall. The performance pitches Yoko's quavering, high pitched vocal gymnastics against Lennon's squelching feedback guitar sounds, with saxophonist John Tchikai and percussionist John Stevens joining in at the end. Yoko's voice gets quite a workout in this piece, which stretches her to the limits and is disturbing and painful to listen to, yet is extremely interesting and challenging music in the avant-garde classical tradition of composers like John Cage. The interplay between her voice and Lennon's guitar is particularly interesting. Lennon's playing as a rhythm guitarist in the Beatles was always the most conceptual music to begin with because rhythm guitarists play alternating and variable patterns. Here, though, Lennon plays nothing but feedback, using Yoko's voice modulations as the only melodic cues. It's some of the best feedback playing ever recorded, ranking with the most creative efforts of such masters of guitar distortion as Jimi Hendrix, Pete Townsend and Jeff Beck.

Side Two of the record is a conceptual piece based around Yoko's hospital stay for complications during her pregnancy that led to her miscarriage. In the first track, "No Bed For Beatle John," she sings about Lennon's desire to stay with her while she was in the hospital, which led to problems because there wasn't a bed available. Lennon eventually got a sleeping bag so he could stay by Yoko's side, all of which is covered in Yoko's vocal. At the end of the song, which is chanted in a semi-liturgical style, John sings softly in counterpoint to Yoko's phrases, recounting hostile press reports about the two and at one point referencing the divorce proceedings that his first wife, Cynthia, had brought against him.

The second track, "Baby's Heartbeat," is exactly that—an amplified recording of the fetus heartbeat inside Yoko as picked up by the hospital's monitoring device. It's particularly poignant, of course, because the baby was never born, but it's also extremely disturbing to listen to, and when the pulsing ends, followed by "Two Minutes of Silence," the cessation of the sound is a tremendous relief that makes the absolute emptiness of the two minutes' meditation vigil even more significant.

The side, and the album, ends with "Radio Play," a very Cage-like idea that describes a quick pattern of radio reception and distortion, which turns the radio signal into unintelligable electronic noise in a hypnotic trance pattern. The side documents Yoko's hospital stay because it was recorded right in the room at Queen Charlotte Hospital on a cassette recording machine.

The cover of the album shows Yoko in her hospital bed, her face twisted in an attitude of extreme pain, with Lennon at her side.

"I was literally in pain," she later explained. "A girl had come up to me and banged my head with her fist. She had a sharp stone hidden in her hand. Another girl pulled my hair. I was also seven months pregnant. I had a miscarriage right after the incident."

Beatles fans were particularly ruthless in their hatred of Yoko, who was generally perceived as being responsible for the Beatles breakup when she was really just helping Lennon realize himself.

"We get all sorts of threatening letters from people advising John that he might have his throat slit for marrying a Japanese. When I was pregnant a girl sent me a little rubber doll filled with pins. You see there was a strong nostalgic feeling for John's previous wife and that had a lot to do with people's feelings for me. Since we were both married before and we suddenly left our previous engagements—people became uptight. For them, our marriage was a moral issue."

Lennon's experience in Canada was so positive he decided to put together an impromptu band under the Plastic Ono banner to appear at a Toronto rock and roll revival show. The show's promoter, John Brower, invited Lennon over just to be there, but John showed up with guitarist Eric Clapton, bassist Klaus Voormann, drummer Alan White and, of course, Yoko.

As other performers at the revival—Bo Diddley, Chicago Transit Authority, Jerry Lee Lewis, Chuck Berry, Doug Kershaw, Lord Sutch, Cat Mother and the All Night Newsboys, Alice Cooper and Gene Vincent—played, traffic in the Detroit to Windsor, Ontario tunnel was backed up as American fans who'd heard of Lennon's plans to play at the festival tried to make it to the site.

Lennon appeared onstage in a white suit and black T-shirt and announced, "We're going to do numbers we know because we never played together before." They opened the set with "Blue Suede Shoes," then played "Money," followed by "Dizzy Miss Lizzy." So much for the rock and roll revival aspect. From there they played Lennon's

"Yer Blues" followed by "Cold Turkey."

After "Cold Turkey" Lennon announced,"This is what we really came here for. I think I know the verses if you know the chorus," and he and Yoko led the audience in a sing-along of "Give Peace A Chance," with Yoko holding aloft the peace sign while they sang.

"Now Yoko is going to do her thing—all over you," said John as he left the stage to Yoko for her performance. She sang, "Don't worry, don't worry, John. Let's hope for peace," as the rest of the band played free form, feedback ridden accompaniment behind her.

Later Lennon was beaming about the show. He had been extremely nervous that it might not come off right and was relieved by how well it worked. "My God," he sighed, "I haven't performed before a large audience for four years. I mean, I did the *Rolling Stones Circus* film with a small audience and I did the Cambridge '69 gig, but they didn't even know I was coming. There were only 200 people there, and they only expected Yoko to arrive anyway.

"We only had time to run through the numbers on the plane coming over, but the band was so funky I couldn't believe it. We did all the old things like 'Blue Suede Shoes' things from the Cavern days in Liverpool. Gene Vincent was standing on the side of the stage crying when we did our number. Backstage he came up to me and whispered 'John, remember Hamburg. Remember all that scene.' "

Lennon had to laugh at some of the problems he encountered in his return to live performance. "The ridiculous thing is that I didn't know any of the lyrics," he said. "When we did 'Money' and 'Dizzy,' I just made up the words as I went along. The band was bashing it out like hell behind me. Yoko came up on stage with us, but she wasn't going to do her bit until we'd done our five songs. Then after 'Money' there was a stop, and I turned to Eric and said, 'What's next?' He just shrugged, so I screamed out, 'C'mon,' and started into something else.

"We did 'Yer Blues' because I've done that with Eric before. It blew our minds. Meanwhile, Yoko had whipped offstage to get some lyrics from her white bag. Then we went into 'Give Peace A Chance' which was just unbelievable. I was making up the words as I went along, I didn't have a clue. After that, we just wandered off to the back of the stage, and we lit up and let go.

"Yoko's first number had a bit of rhythm but the second was completely freaky. It was the sort of thing she did at Cambridge '69 but it was more like Toronto 1974. Yoko just stopped when she'd had enough, walked off and we left all the amps on, going like the clappers. Wow-ow-ow-ow. It went on for another five minutes, just flat. Then Mal Evans went out and turned them off. All the people were singing 'Give Peace A Chance' and it was fantastic. It was bloody marvelous."

The whole thing was recorded and Lennon later said, "We took our cameramen with us, and our business manager, Allen Klein, flew up and made a few quick deals. I understand there's going to be a film of the revival, done by Richard Pennebaker, who did Dylan's *Don't Look Back*. The whole thing was just fantastic, I'm really glad we went. And because of it, we're going to be doing more things like it soon. You get such a great feeling from a gig like that."

The live recording of the event, *The Plastic Ono Band Live Peace In Toronto*, was released on December 12, 1969.

John and Yoko continued to press their efforts for peace and scheduled another Plastic Ono Band appearance. This time the Plastic Ono Band consisted of George Harrison, Eric Clapton, keyboardist Billy Preston, Alan White, Klaus Voormann, and Delaney and Bonnie, who also brought their drummer and horn section. The pre-Christmas concert inspired the band's backdrop, a huge poster which read: "War Is Over! If you want it. Happy Xmas from John and Yoko." The crowd at London's Lyceum Theatre, where the event was held, went wild when the band broke into their opening number, "Cold Turkey."

Lennon sang extremely well on the fifteen minute version of "Cold Turkey," wrenching out some of his best-ever screams. The next and last song was a half-hour rendition of Yoko's "Don't Worry Kyoko." Lennon appeared in a good mood after the show even though the audience exhibited hostile reaction to Yoko. "The Plastic Ono Band is an impromptu thing," he explained when people criticized him for not playing more familiar numbers during the set. "And I'm up there to enjoy myself. The band was digging it—that's what it was about."

The ban on entering the U.S. applied to John and Yoko was lifted temporarily at the beginning of 1970, and they took advantage of the opportunity to enter the States and traveled to Los Angeles, where they underwent therapy prescribed

In May of 1969, John and Yoko greeted Kyoko, Yoko's five-year-old daughter from a previous marriage to film producer Anthony Cox.

Fred Lennon, John's father

The extended family reunites again in July, 1970.
From left are: Yoko Ono, John Lennon, Kyoko,
Yoko's former husband Anthony Cox and his
wife Belinda.

by Dr. Arthur Janov, whose book *The Primal Scream* describes a method of unleashing frustrations which cause problems by screaming and crying to vent supressed emotions. When they completed these therapy sessions John and Yoko returned to England, where they both entered the studio to record their next respective albums.

Lennon's album, *John Lennon*, was stark and powerful. It was the most startling of all the Beatles solo albums. Lennon's nerves had been rubbed raw by the Beatles breakup turmoil and all the abuse heaped upon his relationship with Yoko. The pain was so intense that Lennon admitted he and Yoko had at one point turned to using heroin. "I never injected it or anything," he later explained. "We sniffed a little when we were in real pain. We got such a hard time from everyone, and I've had so much thrown at me, and at Yoko, especially at Yoko. Like Peter Brown in our office, after we came in after six months he comes down and shakes my hand and doesn't even say hello to her. That's going on all the time. And we get into so much pain that we have to do something about it. And that's what happened to us. We took H because of what the Beatles and others were doing to us."

Upon cleaning himself out during his thorough self-analysis with Janov, Lennon had prepared himself mentally to make a record that reflected his pain with such ominous, almost horrifying frenzy that it became an overwhelmingly powerful rock and roll record. For this effort, Lennon sought the services of legendary producer Phil Spector, whose crashingly powerful sound recording techniques helped carve the jagged edges of the record. The opening track, "Mother," begins with somber church bells and evolves into a march-like cadence pushed by stark, crisp drums, an echoing piano rhythm and Lennon's screams for his mother and father, repeated over and over in a rising, blood-curdling frenzy.

"I was watching TV in California," Lennon explained about how he conceptualized the opening, "and there was this old horror movie on, and the bells sounded like that to me. It was probably different, because those were actually bells slowed down that they used on the album. I thought that's how to start 'Mother.' I knew 'Mother' was going to be the first track. Actually I wrote 'Mother' in England."

Opening on such a personal autobiographical note, it was immediately apparent that *John Lennon* was the beginning of a body of work that would be more representative of this great artist than the more famous material he recorded as a Beatle. Even though the second song on the album, "Hold On John," is a much more optimistic tone than the album began on, the starkness of "Mother" sets the mood for the whole record and you end up thinking less about whether Lennon will win the fight that he refers to in "Hold On John" than whether he will be able to sort out what he's fighting and how he intends to take it on.

Lennon's attitude toward the world is revealed in its deepest cynicism on "I Found Out," an intensely paranoid world view in which he discovers that his own existence hurts so much he can hardly be hurt more by the outside world. This is grim stuff, especially when compared to Lennon's pacifist public stance, but it's the result of the excruciating mental housecleaning Lennon had to go through to exorcise the Beatles identity. Beatles, gurus, pop stardom, religions, all of it is a smokescreen, says Lennon in the intensely Bob Dylan influenced "Working Class Hero." Then, in "God," Lennon lays it all on the table, reciting a list of all the pop icons he once swore by that he no longer believes in, ending with the Beatles themselves.

" 'God' was put together from three songs," Lennon later explained. "I had the idea that God is the concept by which we measure pain so that when you have a word like that, you just sit down and sing the first tune that comes into your head and the tune is simple, because I like that kind of music and then I just rolled into it. It was just going on in my head and I got by the first three or four, the rest just came out. I don't know when I realized that I was putting down all these things I didn't believe in. I could have gone on, it was like a Christmas card list: Where do I end? Churchill? Hoover? I thought I had to stop. I was going to leave a gap, and just fill in your own words: Whoever you don't believe in. It had just got out of hand, and Beatles was the final thing because I no longer believe in myth, and Beatles is just another myth.

"I don't believe in it. The dream is over. I'm not just talking about the Beatles, I'm talking about the generation thing. It's over, and we gotta— I have to, personally—get down to so-called reality."

In fact, both John and Yoko's solo albums, which were released at the same time, resulted from the same sessions, the same musicians, and could have just as easily been another double album of Plastic Ono material and would probably been written off as the previous Lennon-Ono efforts had been, but because Lennon's was released seperately people flipped out. This time around, the Plastic Ono Band consisted of Ringo Starr on drums and Klaus Voormann on bass.

Ringo's willingness to play drums on both John and Yoko's material is more than just good nature on his part. It proves that he identified strongly with John's playing and rhythmic conception—the albums' rhythms are starkly powerful, putting the lie to McCartney's post-Beatles assertions that Ringo wasn't much of a drummer and had to be told what to play.

"In spite of all the things," John said about his selection of Ringo for the project, "the Beatles could really play music together when they weren't uptight, and if I get a thing going, Ringo knows where to go, just like that, and he does well. We've played together so long that it fits. That's the only thing I sometimes miss is just being able to sort of blink or make a certain noise and I know they'll all know where we are going on an ad-lib thing.

"But we sold out, you know," Lennon says in his final condemnation of the Beatles. "The music was dead before we went on the theatre tour of Britain. We were feeling shit already, because we had to reduce an hour or two hours' playing, which we were glad about in one way, to twenty minutes, and we would go on and repeat the same twenty minutes every night. The Beatles music died then, as musicians. That's why we never improved as musicians. We killed ourselves then to make it."

The John and Yoko Plastic Ono Band records had virtually identical album covers as well as instrumentation, with one twist. On the back of each record is a childhood picture of the respective artists, while the front cover is a photograph of a large tree in the woods with two small figures sleeping beneath the tree. The picture looks the same on each album—when you reach for the record quickly, it's impossible to tell at a glance which one you have—except that for John's album, Yoko is leaning up against the tree, with John's head on her lap, while on Yoko's cover their positions are reversed.

Yoko's album also contains one track, "Aos," which was not recorded at the same sessions as the rest of the material. It was a tape she made with jazz saxophonist Ornette Coleman for a performance at the Albert Hall in 1968. "Nobody knows there is a point on the first song on Yoko's track," Lennon points out, "where the guitar comes in and even Yoko thought it was her voice, because we did all Yoko's in one night, the whole session. Except for the track with Ornette Coleman from the past that we put on to show people that she wasn't discovered by the Beatles and that she's been around a few years. We got stuff of her with Cage, Ornette Coleman . . . we are going to put out 'Oldies But Goldies' next for Yoko."

The next set of John and Yoko solo albums, which were released a year later, saw each performer moving more toward their traditional means of expression. Yoko's double album, *Fly*, was more experimental sounding, and was tied into a new film of the same name, while Lennon's

In the early seventies, John allowed his Plastic Ono Band activities to lapse. For musical support he turned to both Yoko, and Elephant's Memory. The new troupe lasted several years together.

album, *Imagine*, was easygoing and lyrical when compared to the stark anger of *John Lennon*.

Of all the post-Beatle solo albums, *Imagine* was easily the most satisfying to listen to. The album starts with a floating, timeless feeling as the title track leads off. Lennon's bitterness is cut somewhat this time around as "Crippled Inside" masks his anger in a jovial, honky-tonk facade. "Jealous Guy" is even more effective at turning pain into lyrical beauty. "It's So Hard" follows, a violent, tortured song with lots of echo on the vocal and accompaniment from saxophone master King Curtis. That cut leads into "I Don't Want To Be A Soldier," a song reminiscent of "Well, Well, Well" from Lennon's first album, which pulses along with some great drumming by Alan White underlying a double tracked King Curtis solo.

Side two contains a well publicized attack on Paul McCartney called "How Do You Sleep," as well as a couple of beautiful tunes, "Oh, Yoko," "Oh My Love" and the rocking "Gimme Some Truth."

History is fortunate that both Lennon and Yoko Ono left extensive annotations on the making of *Imagine* and *Fly* thanks to the now departed and much lamented *Crawdaddy* magazine, where I was happy to serve as an editor in the mid '70s. Lennon gave a track by track analysis of the making of *Imagine*: " 'Imagine': A song conceived in my head without melody. The first verse came to me very quickly in the form of a childlike street-chant: *da da da da dadee dee da dee da ee a eeeh*. The piano intro I've had hanging around in my head for a few years—the chords and melody followed naturally from this. The middle eight was conceived to finish off the song, I think it works as a song. Of course, there is always room for improvement—otherwise I wouldn't make anymore. The third verse came to me in an eight-seater plane. It's a song for children.

" 'Crippled Inside': Arrived in bed with nary a thought to whether it was 'done before,' 'witty,' or such like bullshit. 'One thing you can't hide is when you're crippled inside' came complete with melody. The rest I just filled in. The middle eight melody is from some old traditional song I heard a few years ago. It fits well. We did it in one take—it shows—it swings. Klaus plays beautiful stand up bass.

" 'Jealous Guy': The melody came from a 'cod' '30s type idea I had a few years ago (India). I never did anything with it but always liked the melody. The words were silly, anyway, I sang it to Yoko—Phil and a few people and they always winced. I decided to change it—and with Yoko's help I did. I don't believe these tight-skinned people who are 'never jealous.' Nicky Hopkins' piano is beautifully busked as is the bass and drums, et. al. Result—'Jealous Guy.'

" 'It's So Hard': I like to sing blues-rock or whatever it is, the words were written with *the sound* in mind rather than meaning. Although both are useful. I also like playing guitar. This was the first finished record I made at Ascot studios in our home, we didn't have any limiters at the time etc.—but it sounded all right to me! King Curtis (who was killed a week later R.I.P.) and the Flux Fiddlers were overdubbed at the Record Plant New York, everyone calls them 'easter'—they're just violins playing guitar parts!

" 'Soldier': Started off in the 'Working Class Hero' days, finished virtually in the studio. It has a peculiar rhythm and Jim Keltner and the rest of them do a fantastic job keeping up. Another first take (obviously). The words are lost or wrong sometimes and I also sing it in many keys at once. But it still has a nice feel—it depends on what mood I'm in, liking it or not. Yoko sticks up for it! (Each song takes on a personality when it is finished and we get possessive!)

" 'Truth': Another 'oldie' (India again) with words finished recently. I was wondering what truth I was after in India. George does a sharp solo with his steel finger (he's not too proud of it—but I like it). I like the overall sound on this track tho' I'm not sure if I'd go out and buy it.

" 'Oh My Love': A joy to write and a joy to sing and record! Written by Yoko—based on her original lyric—we finished it very quickly one late night together. The beginning of the melody being started last year. Writing songs is like writing books—you store little melodies/words/ideas in your mind library and fish them out when you need them.

" 'How Do You Sleep': I know you'll all be wondering about this one! It's been around since late '69 in a similar form to this—but not quite (i.e. more abstract). I'd always envisioned that heavy kind of beat for it and wanted to record it, whatever the lyric turned out to be. When I heard Paul's messages in *Ram*—(yes there are dear reader!) Too many people going where? Missed our lucky what? What was *our* first mistake? 'Can't be wrong.' Huh! I mean, Yoko, me and *other friends* can't *all be hearing things*. So to have some fun, I must thank Allen Klein publicly for the 'line' just another day. A real poet! Some people don't see the funny side of it at all. Too bad. What am I supposed to do, make you laugh? It's what you might call an 'angry letter' only sung—get it? George Harrison's best solo to date on this cut—as good as anything I've heard from anyone—anywhere. I'm singing sharp again—but me rhythm guitar makes up for it. A good 'live' session from all the band. I don't think about Paul this way, every moment of my life, in case you're wondering.

" 'How': George's favorite song. I'm proud to say. (He also digs the strings on 'It's So Hard'— maybe a few of his fans will follow his taste and buy it! Heh! Heh!) The verses were written last year. Middle eight was written during the recording session (my favorite bit, it's new to me you see) wish I'd sung it better but it's a nice tune, it was hard doing the breaks. Mellow.

" 'Oh Yoko': An easy come easy go song—like whistling down the lane to meet your lover. She's mine and I'm always singing/thinking/being about her—it came naturally, we did one take and enjoyed it. Phil and me croaked on the backing 'chorus' later. I always do the wrong songs first— so when it's time to sing softly—I've wrecked my throat rocking! I'll never learn—'Twist and Shout' was recorded at the end of a twelve-hour session. Jesus, what torture (old man's reminiscences.) That's all folks, if you like it, listen to it, if you don't, shutup.

"I'd just like to add a special thanks to this month's Plastic Ono Band: Yoko, Phil, Klaus (whose bass playing has yet to be recognized) Jim,

Alan, George and all the other people involved. All in all it was a good nine day session (6 in U.K. and 3 in N.Y.). One day less than the last album. With a regular nuclear group—we could get verrrrry fast.

"P.S. Congratulations to Paul and Linda from the both of us."

In these remarks Lennon's humility and sense of humor are well represented, not to mention his frankness. As usual, Yoko's comments on *Fly* were downright illuminating, crucial source material for listening to and understanding her record, almost like the contextual notes accompanying her conceptual pieces.

" 'Fly' is the last track of the record but it was made first," she wrote, "just when my last album was finished and was out in the street. It was made in our bedroom in the Regency Hotel in N.Y., Xmas 1970, on a Nagra operated by John. I was thinking that I must make a soundtrack for my film *Fly* which was just near completion. Then John suggested maybe we should knock it off before the 10 o'clock news that night. It was that casual. We did it in one take, as most of my things are done.

"I don't believe in doing things over. When I was painting one day it suddenly occurred to me that there is no line that you can go over. If you go over a line, the line you went over is a totally new line.

"When you use correctocopy to correct typing mistakes, you don't go over the wrong letters with the right letters. With the correctosheet you have to first go over the same line again with the exact wrong letters you typed before. Only then can you erase the mistakes and type over the correct letters. I'm always fascinated by this seemingly illogical fact.

"It looks like there is some philosophical connection between these stories but I don't seem to be able to find the word for it now. The point is, I don't believe in doing things over, and unless it is a really bad take, I believe in the first take.

"Another story: This is about a Japanese painter who was asked by his lord to do a painting. The lord waited a year yet nothing came of his request. He sent a messenger to the painter. The painter came out and said, 'Oh, okay, just a minute,' or something and did a one stroke painting while the messenger was waiting in the next room. The messenger returned with the painting and told the lord what had happened. The lord was very angry and arrested the painter. 'You insulted me by making me wait for a whole year for the painting and on top of that, you used only a second to finish the painting. What was that!' The painter calmly replied, 'Every day of the year that I was not painting, I was preparing for the painting. The painting may have been one stroke and it may have taken only a second to do, but the whole year of pain and joy were in that stroke. The year was a necessary time.'

"I used to do things, for example, fast, five days before a concert to prepare my mind for the performance because the performance was not my skill but the state of mind I was in at the time. Whenever I pick up a mike, I'm aware that every minute of thirty-eight years goes into it, whether I like it or not.

"What I did in *Fly* was what I wanted to do for

153

ten years, so I was very satisfied when I did it. I thought of making an album around this piece. It took almost a whole year after that to finally complete the album, though. Another Xmas is coming very soon. The winter is cold and tough—and you have to crawl a long way before you fly. Winter is age. Cold makes you go slow. *Fly* is a monologue in three stages.

"Section One—monologue:

"Section Two—monologue in a dialogue form:

"John played his guitar against the playback of my voice from section one. The guitar tape was then reversed and put together with my voice tape, so that the voice and the guitar ran in two opposite directions as separate monologues.

"Section Three—monologue in a trialogue form: John played his guitar against the reversed playback of the section two. John's guitar tape made in this way was reversed and played while I did my voice. When the guitar tape was over and when my voice was still going, John played the radio against my voice.

" 'Monologue' is a reminiscence of my old days. I used to search for musicians who had the same state of mind as I to make musical dialogues with. But I had never met anyone who could really do that with me on the level that I was thinking of. Female artists for some reason, didn't have enough experience in expressing themselves with instruments—maybe they were more accustomed to using a direct instrument which is one's own body—while the male artists were caught in whatever brilliance they possessed and were not free. So I ended up always doing a monologue. John is the first person I met who knows how to be

154

free, and that is why he plays such an important role in all of my pieces. For instance, you see that section three of *Fly* is a guitar solo with voice accompaniment rather than the other way around.

"Most of the pieces in this album are centered around a dialogue between my voice and John's guitar. John and I crawl, roll and fly together. John brought in musicians that are fine samurais. John, as a rhythm guitarist, leads the rhythm track, he pushes them, drops them, chases them and frees them. He makes it easy for them to fly with me. Listen to Ringo and Jim Keltner's drumming, Klaus Voormann's bass, Chris Osborne's guitar and listen to the intricate conversation that goes on among all of us in 'Mind Train.' Chris Osborne came from a guitar shop to sell a guitar to John. He stayed and played.

"I was always fascinated by the idea of making special instruments for special emotions—instruments that lead us to emotions arrived at by their own motions rather than by our control. With those instruments, I wanted to explore emotions and vibrations which have not been explored as yet in music. I thought of building a house on a hill which makes different sounds by the wind that goes through different windows, doors and holes. (Re: *Grapefruit*: paperback edition out now!!!) Ten years ago I met Joe Jones who's been making such instruments almost unnoticed. This time, Joe built me eight new instruments specifically for this album which can play by themselves with minimum manipulation (turning switches only.)

"I'm very happy with what happened with 'Airmale' and 'You' as a result of my session with Tone Deaf Music Co. 'Airmale' is Yang and 'You' is Yin. 'Don't Connect the Waves' is the water that connects the two Yin and Yang islands. 'Airmale' expresses the delicateness of male. 'You' expresses the aggressiveness of female. 'You' has all the feminine resentment; moaning and satisfaction in it. Finally, there is just a wind blowing over a sand hill over white dried female bones, but still, with emotion. A wind created with tape feedback is what I always wanted to do; a rock number with a tape loop of feedback as a riff. But this will do for now.

"When I was at Sarah Lawrence, which was before I joined the avant-garde, and in London around 1967–8, which was when I was feeling very miserable, I composed many songs. 'Mrs. Lennon' is in that category of songs, but unlike 'Remember Love' and 'Who Has Seen the Wind,' I felt it was recorded very well. 'Mrs. Lennon' was meant to be a joke on me, and also an anti-war song. The lyrics were written in 1969 and the music was finished this month in New York during the recording session.

" 'Midsummer New York' is about the deep insecurity that I have in me that I associate with my life in New York before I met John. The lyrics were made last year, though I always wanted to make a song that uses the word 'shaking' with a double meaning, as I discovered the use of the word in rock songs in 1968.

"This album roughly turned out to be: First and Second sides: songs to dance to—rock songs with a physical beat. Third and fourth sides: songs to listen to—mind music with a mind beat. The Mind Music Section has number connections:

'Fly'—1, 2 and 3
'Airmale'—5
'Don't Count the Waves'—7
'You'—9

"It is very important to know about numbers made to understand the connections among the pieces, so I will quote the relevant lines from my writing called ' On Number, ' and end this long introduction to the album.

"ONE

"One is an immobile number. One is found in our bodies often as fixed parts. We count ourselves as one but it might be better to count oneself as half a pair or a half when you think of the fact that our reproductive organs can only function by meeting the other half.

"One step is only half a move. Since we have two legs we have to take two steps or jump in order to move from one position to the next. One is before the cell splits in two. It is only mobile in the process of becoming two. One as a force is a point—which does not extend like a line. One constantly seeks for states of zero and two.

"TWO

"Two is a state that is mobile by nature. Like the footstep that goes one, two. It moves from one position to the next. Two as a force is a line. It extends and unlike one, does not have to move to become mobile. Two is a state after the splitting of the cell. Two constantly seeks for the state of one and three. We find two in our bodies quite often as a pair. Two is our heartbeat. After one and two, all the numbers are a combination of one and two. Therefore, there are only three basic states of numbers in the world: one, two and three, which is a combination of one and two.

"THREE

"Three is a number we cannot find in our bodies but we find it in nature around us. I call it a time number because we use it to divide time and the days. When the heart beats in three, it is because the heart is moving faster than what is natural. The heart beats one, two, one, two. And one number out of this repetition of two gets abbreviated because of the speed. That is three. That means we set the time to the number that is one beat faster than our natural heartbeat. No wonder the culture is suffering from accelerated speed. The world will slow down if you dispense with clocks and watches and just follow your heartbeat.

"The natural rhythm, when you don't check or control it consciously, always goes slower (towards four) or faster (towards two) than a clock. Three is very fast and very mobile. It is a running rhythm as opposed to the walking rhythm of two, four and eight. Three as a force is a three dimensional point—an exclamation mark. Three will always seek for state of two or state of four. In three, two (which is a mobile number) and one (which is an immobile number) exist together equally. Paradox makes three extremely active toward the inside, but not very active outside. While two is a traveling number, three is a whirling number (it moves toward spirally). After three, all numbers are combination of states of one, two and three.

"FIVE

"Five is a number that very rarely exists on earth but exists very much in the sky (such as the points of stars—but you know that even the five points of stars actually do not exist). Unlike one (0 & 2), two (4 & 8) and three (6 & 9), five has no corresponding numbers in the series. In this sense it is very similar to 7.

"In our bodies, it exists only on our hands and feet—as if that is the sign from the sky in us. The parts of our bodies where five exist are the only parts that have something to do with physical connections to things outside our bodies. Our hands reach to other things and our feet take us to other places with the help of a traveling number (2). Five is a connection number—and just as the fingers do not work unless the thumb moves in an opposite direction from the rest of the fingers, five will be immobile unless it has different or opposite elements (one, two and three) in it.

"SEVEN

"Seven is a conceptual number. Seven, like five, is a number you cannot find in our bodies (more so than five), or in the nature around us. I call it a conceptual number or number of music because we divide the musical scale into seven. (In time, we can only see it in the division of the week.) And like five, it has no corresponding numbers.

"NINE

"Nine is a corresponding number of three and six. Nine is superactive. Specially, it is the closest of the numbers to a circle. As a force it has a spirally forward movement as does three.

"But despite all the words, music itself exists somewhere else and was made by pure instinct (*That goes for me, too*, J. L.) and nothing else. Flashes of imagery and emotion."

Upon the release of *Imagine* Lennon began what was to be the last portion of his life, his stay in the adopted home of New York City. John and Yoko were obviously very fond of New York at this time and spent their days hanging out and making new friends around town. The two were made to feel at home by several notable New York street people and a couple of fans left over from the radical political climate of the late '60s. Jerry Rubin and Abbie Hoffman were Lennon's political contacts, and although Lennon was fairly good-natured in his attempts to befriend them and find out what they were about, the mere association with radical leaders was interpreted in conservative political quarters as tantamount to conspiracy and Lennon was to suffer for his friendship with these people later.

The other new friend they started hanging out with in New York was David Peel, a street singer who played for free in Washington Square and the East Village all the time and started to introduce Lennon and Ono to other underground musicians around town.

John and Yoko also decided to make an impromptu appearance at the legendary Fillmore East in New York's Lower East Side. The two showed up at a Frank Zappa concert to jam in June of 1971 with Zappa's Mothers of Invention. They played a hard edged funk tune, "You Know I Love You Baby," which Lennon introduced by saying, "This is a song I used to sing when I was

John and Yoko walk briskly to their chartered executive jet at Gatwick Airport. Both were en route to their home in Surrey after a car crash in Scotland. John's injuries—hidden by his beard—required 17 stitches; Yoko needed 14.

in the Cavern at Liverpool. I haven't done it since, so . . ." Lennon went on to play a spirited rock and roll song as Yoko sang with her warbling vocal style meshing nicely with Lennon's guitar. Then Yoko and one of Zappa's keyboardists engaged in an interesting vocal-instrumental exchange before the band switched into playing a new, impromptu riff song called "Scumbag," during which Lennon screamed authoritatively while Zappa played a great guitar solo behind the vocal. The jam ended with Yoko singing over a feedback accompaniment reminiscent of "Cambridge '69," and this time the audience loved it, roaring approval for Yoko's experimental music.

After the Zappa gig Lennon was encouraged to try and put together a road show once more. Jerry Rubin introduced him to a funky New York based R & B band called Elephant's Memory, which Lennon liked and decided to play some gigs with and use for his next record. "I've been practicing with Elephant's Memory," Lennon said at the time. "They're a New York band, good musicians. I really like them. They understand everything that's going on, too. I'm going to play with them on the Mike Douglas show. Seems to keep changing, though. I'd like to have some of the people who played on the (*Imagine*) album, too. I'd like to have two drummers, like a lot of bands have now. Jim Keltner's coming into town and I'm gonna explain the situation to him. I think he'll be up for it when he sees that things are becoming firmer."

Lennon used Elephant's Memory and Keltner for *Some Time In New York City*, which was the most overtly political album he ever made. The cover of the record is a mocked up newspaper with

162

the title as the paper's logo and the songs with their lyrics laid out as the stories in the paper. Many of the songs were direct comments on current events: Lennon's campaign to free John Sinclair, who'd been imprisoned for ten years for the possession of two joints of marijuana ("John Sinclair"); Irish liberation ("Sunday Bloody Sunday" and "The Luck of the Irish"); Woman's liberation ("Woman Is the Nigger of the World"); prison reform ("Attica State", "Born In A Prison"); Angela Davis ("Angela"). The record was a two disc set with the second disc made up of jams from the UNICEF show and with Zappa's band.

Some Time In New York City was a rough edged, home-made sounding record, but the newspaper format was ingenious because it was a very immediate reflection of Lennon's concerns and observations on the world at the time he recorded it. In a sense it may have been *too* honest, though, for the critics panned it for not being slick enough and the authorities used it as additional reason to keep Lennon out of the country as an undesirable alien. The visa granting him the right to stay in the country temporarily was about to expire and the efforts to get him out were escalating. What's more, the single released from the album, "Woman Is the Nigger of the World," was banned by many radio stations which considered it too political.

"At first we thought the record was being banned because of the word nigger," Lennon pointed out, "but since the record came out we spoke to all our black friends including the people who run *Ebony* and *Jet* which are the biggest black magazines. They're fully behind us."

Lennon attributed his newfound high spirits to Yoko's influence on him. "It's like having a mother and everything. That's it. So I'm secure in my relationship with her so I can afford to relax. I was never relaxed before. I was always uptight."

New York itself also got some of the credit for Lennon's renewed spirits. "I wrote 'New York City,'" he explained, "but it's like wherever Yoko and I lived we were going pretty fast in our lives. It was like we were a little miniature New York City in London or something, but this is the only place where everybody is going at the same speed as us, which is good. So it's like instead of going against the waves which we'd been doing a lot of the time. In New York you go with the waves, they're all going with you. It's that kind of inspiring thing and there's just so many great people here apart from the stars that live here, you know the great artists of music and of straight art, just all the people are much groovier here. It's the hippest place on earth and that's why it's really inspiring to be here and it just makes you wanna rock like crazy."

Lennon went on to explain his shifting songwriting perspective on *Some Time* . . . "I think if you get down to basics whatever the problem is, it's usually to do with love. People's neurotic need for love. So I think 'All You Need Is Love' is a true statement. I'm not saying 'all we have to do is to . . .' because 'All You Need' came out in the Flower Power generation time, it doesn't mean that all you have to do is put on a phoney smile or wear a flower dress and it's gonna be all right. Love is not just something that you stick on posters or stick on the back of your car or on the back of your jacket or on a badge. I'm talking about real love so I still believe that. Love is appreciation of other people and allowing them to be. Love is allowing somebody to be themselves and that's what we do need. Even with a tough thing like 'Attica,' which we both wrote together, we're saying things like 'Rockefeller pulled the trigger,' whatever it is, but we are still saying, 'all they want is truth and justice, all they need is love and care,' it's still the basic underlying thing as love. Although maybe two or four years ago, maybe I was so pacifist that I wouldn't even believe in self-defense, but, I do believe in self-defense."

Lennon went on to say that the political nature of *Some Time* . . . happened naturally. "We finished it on March 20th which is our third wedding anniversary. The morning we finished it was the dawn of the night we finished remixing the final thing and we didn't know and she turned around and said: 'You know what day this is? It's March 20th!' Wow! And so we put that on the cover. It's not a particularly new idea, incorporating the lyrics like that, and there was nothing else for us to do. When you hear the record, and you see the lyrics, you understand it's all about current affairs and there's no other way to present it but as a newspaper. And that's what we've done.

"This is the first pop album we've made together although we made sort of avant-garde albums together and on all Yoko's albums I've been backing her and on all my albums she's usually there somewhere on a drum or a tambourine or singing or she looks after my voice side of it. I can't do anything without her. But this is the first time we've done a pop album together and she's singing like teeny bopper stuff, 'Sisters Oh Sisters.' Half the songs we wrote together and half we wrote separately.

"Since I know a lot of people are going to say, 'Oh John and Yoko have gone political and that's it and everything is gonna be political,' so we can say upfront now that, see, Yoko wrote 'Sisters Oh Sisters' first and I thought it was great and I was sitting around thinking 'Wow!' and then I remembered she'd said this 'Woman Is the Nigger of the World' and at that time I was arguing with her a bit, saying, 'Well, what about black slaves and what about the men that did this.' But all the time she said, 'All the time there was the woman there too. Never forget, whatever the men were going through the woman was there going through it with him or was left behind if he was hung, with the kids. Whatever it was, the woman suffered even more, usually. So gradually I understood that and then after she wrote 'Sisters Oh Sisters' I was saying, 'Wow, you know "Sisters Oh Sisters" is great, but you really said it that time with "Woman Is the Nigger of the World." ' And I said, 'Can I write it with you? I know it's your statement, but I remembered, right? So can we write it together?' And she said, 'Yeah.' So then we wrote 'Attica State' which is months and months ago, but we never did an electric recording of it. So we did 'Attica State' and Yoko immediately gets inspired to do 'Born In A Prison' or something because we were singing about Attica. So then they started all coming out like that and that's why they all started to have the same kind of themes. And then we'd written 'The Luck of the Irish' like last October and we sent out the lyrics and a sort of bedroom version with an acoustic guitar to a few underground stations and a few underground papers and some in Europe as well, just to get the lyrics out and the idea out and it wasn't until now that we produced a sort of, you know, with violins and a whole band playing. It turned out well, actually.

"So then 'Sunday Bloody Sunday' happened much later. When they killed the thirteen people. So we wrote that the day after kind of thing. Practically the same day Paul was writing 'Give Ireland Back to the Irish.' But 'Luck of the Irish' was long before that. I think Paul's Irish song and 'Sunday Bloody Sunday' must have been written almost the same night because it was right after it happened. So it was like we were connected like that. Same night. I bet he and Linda was doing it exactly the same time as us probably. So then it went on, ending up with two songs about Ireland. Then we got a request, 'Will you please write a song about Angela?' from the Angela Davis people. So there, now how do you write a song about somebody you don't really know? It's the same as 'John Sinclair.' Y'know, I don't really know him so I try to write it in a sort of universal way, not too personal. All I'm saying is, 'It ain't fair, John Sinclair.' It could be anybody that's in prison. So with 'Angela' too we tried to keep away from the political side and the detail of it and just treat her as a human being who's stuck away.

"The funny story about it is like we do the Sinclair thing and he gets out and he would have got out anyway probably, but it just sort of like magically he gets out at the same time. Well I don't know, I mean it must have been coming anyway. So we get this request for Angela, but they sent it to England so it must have come about three weeks later. We write the song, we get into the studio that night to record it. That day she's been released! We just get into the studio and everybody comes running and says, 'She's out!' We said, 'Well we were going to sing it anyway, it still means something.' So we still made the record. So that's the problem with doing current affairs on record. A record takes so long to come out that the current affairs is all over then, but we think this one sustains anyway.''

After *Some Time In New York City* the attempt to oust Lennon from the country was stepped up. During the making of his next album, *Mind Games*, Lennon faced deportation and had to go to court to be granted a stay in order to finish the recording.

The case was complicated by the fact that Yoko was trying to locate the whereabouts of her daughter, Kyoko, by her previous marriage to Anthony Cox. In early 1972 Yoko was awarded custody of the child by a Houston court under the condition that she and John had to live in the country. Yoko maintained the deportation procedures were ''really unjust and cruel treatment'' because ''they are forcing me to choose either my husband or my child.''

''We both love the Village and New York City and really want to stay,'' Yoko went on. ''We feel we're being kicked out of our own town.''

Yoko claimed that Cox and his second wife, Melinda, had kidnapped Kyoko and were hiding her. "My former husband has said," she stated, " 'All we have to do is hide until they leave'."

For the next two years, while he was in the process of recording two more albums, *Walls and Bridges* and *Rock and Roll*, Lennon fought a see-saw battle in the courts to stay in the country. He made a public issue of the case, appearing on talk shows and outlining his plight in a number of interviews. He explained how the drug conviction the case was based on came about on the *Tomorrow* show:

"In the late '60s there was a head-hunting cop who was not very high up in the drug department in London, which was pretty new anyway, they had two dogs for the whole department. And he went round to bust every pop star he could get his hands on and really got famous. Some of the pop stars had dope in the house and some of them didn't; it didn't matter to him. He planted it or whatever. That's what he did to me. At that time I didn't have any drugs.

"He's in jail now, by the way, because he made it up to be top dog and he had a big drug scandal which happened after I left and he was caught in Australia.

"I'd just moved into an apartment and I had everything from the old apartment all over the place so I thought maybe this was a bit of hash that was left over. I just copped a plea—I thought it was only a hundred dollars or so. But at any rate the guy had planted me and I didn't find out until later when I called a few friends and said, 'Did you have stuff?' And they said, 'I did have stuff, it was right there on the table and they didn't notice it. They planted a pound in the bedroom.'

"I did just pay the fine and that was the end of it. So I came to America for a visit and decided to live here."

Other people had other ideas, however. Senator Strom Thurmond had reportedly sent a memorandum to the Justice Department urging them to see that Lennon was deported, a directive that apparently made it all the way down to the level of the local immigration department in New York. They had set a legal snare for Lennon but when the trap was sprung the resulting publicity weakened their case. Nevertheless, even though Lennon eventually sidestepped the deportation, the whole procedure took its toll, distracting him from his work and at one point disrupting his relationship with Yoko.

"I try to forget about it," he later said, "and keep my head buried in my work. But there was a period, about eighteen months ago, when it was really beginning to get to me because it just wouldn't go away. It's like a fly—only worse—it just won't go away. And then you forget about it and I think, 'Now it must be all right because the lawyer hasn't called me for a bit,' and then suddenly I was in the middle of making an album— *Walls and Bridges*—and I was in a taxicab going to the Record Plant where I make the records in New York and it came over the air: 'John Lennon has thirty days to get out.' So I just jokingly said to the cab driver, 'Okay drive me to the airport.' Cause nobody had told me . . . because they didn't want to interfere with my work."

It was impossible to insulate Lennon from having to appear in court on his own behalf, though. "It was physically getting to me," he later said. "I was so paranoid from them tapping the phone and following me . . . I was ready to go on the road (with Elephant's Memory) for pure *fun*. I didn't want to go on the road for money. That was the time when I was standing up in the Apollo with a guitar at the Attica relatives' benefit or ending up on the stage at the John Sinclair rally. I felt like going on the road and playing music. And whatever excuse—charity or whatever—would have done me. But they kept pulling me back into court. I had the group hanging around, but finally I had to say, 'Hey, you better get on with your lives.' Now, the last thing on earth I want to do is perform. That's a direct result of the immigration thing."

Another result was that Lennon now felt that he had been steered wrong for the *Some Time In New York City* project. "I got off the boat, only it was an airplane, and landed in New York, and the first people who got in touch with me was Jerry Rubin and Abbie Hoffman. It's as simple as that. And the next thing you know I'm doing John Sinclair benefits and one thing and another. I'm pretty movable, as an artist, you know. They almost greeted me off the plane and the next minute I'm involved.

"It became journalism, not poetry," he said of his work at that time. "And I basically feel that I'm a poet. I realized that we were poets, but we were really folk poets, and rock and roll was folk poetry. Then I began to take it seriously on another level, saying, 'Well, I am reflecting what's going *on*, right?' And then I was making an *effort* to reflect what was going on. Well, it doesn't work like that."

It was about this time also that Lennon left Yoko for an extended period. Though he never directly attributed it to the mental strain caused by his court battles, he admitted that the whole period was indecipherable to him. "It started, somehow, at the end of '73, going to do this *Rock and Roll* album. It had quite a lot to do with Yoko and I, whether I knew it or not, and then suddenly I was out on my own. Next thing I'd be waking up drunk in strange places, or reading about myself in the paper, doing extraordinary things, half of which I'd done and half of which I hadn't done. And find myself in a mad *dream* for a year. I'd been in many mad dreams, but this, it was pretty wild."

During this time Lennon had moved to Los Angeles temporarily to do some recording and spent a lot of time in the company of Harry Nilsson. Their exploits of drunkenness and shenanigans kept the rock gossip mills running for over a year. Lennon and Nilsson were running a Laurel-and-Hardy routine from coast to coast, their most notorious appearances coming at L.A.'s Troubadour night club. They showed up for opening night of the Smothers Brothers' comeback attempt. When the Smothers Brothers, who were friends with John and Harry, took the stage, they received some good-natured razzing from the drunken pair. Hard, forced laughter followed each gag, and the audience grew strangely silent, more interested in watching an ex-Beatle perform than the Smothers Brothers. Smobro manager Kenny Craig, worried that the group was being upstaged, tried to quiet the two down but couldn't, and club owner Doug Weston ended up throwing them out.

Lennon had preceded this incident with another

bit of outrageousness at the same club when he appeared wearing a Kotex on his head. He asked a waitress, "Do you know who I am?" and she replied "Yeah, you're some shmuck wearing a Kotex on his head."

"I think it's a good remark," Lennon later said about the waitress's comment, "and so what?" As for the Smothers Brothers episode, all Lennon would say was, "It was my first night on Brandy Alexanders and my last."

In 1975 Lennon's life stabilized after his year long "dream." The personal and legal problems that had been dogging him for the decade since he decided that he no longer wanted to be a Beatle were finally resolved. The last settlement of the Beatles legal battle was arrived at, freeing Lennon legally to record under his own name exclusively once and for all with no attachment to the remains of the Beatles empire. His immigration status was also cleared up and he was able to stay in the U.S. without worrying about official harassment.

Most importantly, Lennon reunited with Yoko Ono and the two began a blissful five years of domestic solitude at the Dakota. Yoko took over management of their business affairs while John cared for and doted on their newborn son Sean.

When Lennon returned from his half-decade-long retirement in 1980 he was a happy man. For the first time in his scrappy, hard-fought life, he had set himself aside enough time to just be himself, with none of the demands of the recording industry or stardom to deal with. This was the ultimate act of defiance, to insist that his own private life, getting to know his child, baking bread, just hanging around the house if he wanted to, was every bit as important as being a Beatle.

Double Fantasy reflected these concerns directly. "Starting Over" and "Clean Up Time" were Lennon's accounts of his new lifestyle, "Beautiful Boy" a love song to his son, and the chilling exchange between his "I'm Losing You" and Yoko's "I'm Moving On" an account of the repercussions of their separation. "Watching the Wheels" states his case forcefully for a personal life being more important than the life of a star.

"We got back together," Lennon explained in a recent interview, "decided this was our life, that having a baby was important to us and that anything else was subsidiary to that."

And so John Lennon was granted his wish. He finally got the chance to enjoy part of his life completely on his own terms before it was so swiftly and cruelly ended. He left behind a few more songs in various states of completion, as well as a rag and bone shop of poems, lyrics and fiction bits in his notebooks. There are a number of live performances which may or may not ever be released. The only remaining mystery about his music comes from a remark he made in one of the last interviews before his retirement in 1975. He told Pete Hammill in a *Rolling Stone* piece that he had just started to write a new album, which he said was perhaps half finished. Perhaps some of this material exists in some form somewhere.

THE
END

MARK DAVID CHAPMAN WAS BORN MAY 10, 1955 IN
Fort Worth, Texas. His father is David Curtis
Chapman and his mother is listed as Diane
Elizabeth Pease Chapman. At the time of Mark's
birth, his father was in the Air Force. More than
likely, Mark's father was serving at the Carswell
Air Force base which is near to Fort Worth.
Although much of the Chapmans' early years are
shrouded in mystery, it is known that the elder
Chapman achieved some success in the energy field
as an executive at Amoco, a petroleum giant.

When Mark was a teenager, the Chapman
family was living in the Decatur, Georgia area.
Mark attended Columbia High School in Decatur.
Chapman's father remembers that his son loved
the Beatles. In fact, "He collected every album
they've ever made . . . since he was a little boy,"
the father recalls.

Mark was heavily into music as a teenager. His
father had taught him to play the box guitar when
the boy was only seven years old, so it's not surprising that he ended up playing guitar in a rock
and roll band when he was in high school. He even

wore his hair in the early Beatle 'mop-top' style.

Even at that time Mark appeared to be pulled in too many directions. Chapman graduated from Columbia High School in 1973; a classmate, who is now a Baptist minister, Rev. Walter Newton Hendrix Jr., remembers the dichotomies of Chapman's teen years this way: "Mark wasn't wild, but he had that hood look about the ninth or tenth grade." He continued, "You know, long hair, old Army jackets, that kind of thing. Then he changed." Hendrix indicated that after those years Chapman changed by becoming deeply Christian and carrying a Bible and a "Jesus Notebook" with him.

Not much is known about Chapman's mother; it is assumed that she is living in Hawaii and may have even lent Mark money to come to New York. Tammy Morris, a friend from high school, recalls her impression of Mrs. Chapman in the early years by saying that Mark's mother was a real disciplinarian who "hollered at Mark a lot." His mother often accused him of being on drugs and was often "searching his room and putting him on restriction," Morris recalls.

In Decatur Mark began his long association with the Young Men's Christian Association. From 1969–1973 he was a counselor at the 'Y' and was reportedly very effective with the younger children. It seems he was most interested in warning them about the evils of drug use. He supposedly used his own experiences as examples of how bad things could get. "He was a regular Pied Piper with the children," said Vince Smith, an Atlanta YMCA executive who had known Chapman as a counselor in Decatur.

Chapman attended DeKalb Junior College for a time after his graduation from high school, but the most notable influence in his life was his deepening relationship with the YMCA. Soon after the Lennon killing, an official from the YMCA in North Carolina called Chapman's father at his Chamblee, Georgia home and indicated that Chapman was one of the finest representatives that the 'Y' had ever had. Chapman's first noteworthy project for the YMCA was a trip that took him to Lebanon in the Mideast. This strange venture took Mark to Beirut in the midst of some of the heaviest fighting in that country's civil war. Oddly, Mark had been sent there at that chaotic time to set up a YMCA youth hostel in the middle of strife-torn Beirut. At that point Chapman's father was still with Amoco. He released an Amoco Oil Company newsletter that announced his son's voyage to Beirut. The headline read: "Chapman's Son Survives Shootout." The story described how Chapman survived the hostilities but was unable to get the hostel open. It went on to add, however, that Chapman had managed to record the heavy machine gun fire between the warring factions.

Chapman returned to the states in deep depression over his failure to get the hostel going. The YMCA reassigned Chapman to Fort Chaffee in Arkansas where they had a group center aimed at helping Vietnamese refugees who had escaped the conflagration in Southeast Asia. There is a wealth of photographs that show Chapman frolicking happily with Vietnamese children on the grounds of Fort Chaffee.

Gregg Lyman, 27, a co-worker at Fort Chaffee, described Chapman as "an outgoing, good humored, optimistic guy" who "never really lost his temper."

David Moore, 40, Executive Director of the Duncan YMCA in Chicago, was a good friend to Chapman and once shared an apartment with him. Moore alleged that upon his return from overseas, Chapman was troubled, and that one of the outlets that he sought was drugs. Moore also indicates that Chapman was not happy in his home life in his teens and that he apparently was driven to running away more than once, and that he initially drifted into experimenting with drugs at that point. "He was into the drug scene and had done some barbiturates and amphetamines and maybe even heroin," Moore alleges. "But then he met this woman who changed his life."

The woman was named Jessica and she apparently convinced Chapman that drugs were absolutely the wrong thing for him. This was during the time that the joyful pictures of Chapman were taken at Fort Chaffee. Jessica also convinced Chapman to make the final commitment of his life to Jesus, and under Jessica's guidance Chapman became "Born Again."

"He was madly in love with Jessica and she kind of straightened him around." Moore said. "She made him a Christian."

In 1975 Fort Chaffee was closed as a refugee center. There was a vacuum in Chapman's life after the center closed, and Jessica convinced him to fill it by enrolling in a nearby Bible school, Covenant College, a small Reform Presbyterian school located in Lookout Mountain, Tennessee. Apparently Chapman was not cut out for the academic life and that precipitated a calamity for him.

Chapman couldn't hack the school work and flunked out at the end of one semester. Jessica became disgusted with him at this point and cut their relationship dead. In the intensity of his love for Jessica, Chapman became extremely depressed.

Moore remembers the period this way: "He was a real bright kid who just didn't have the discipline," Moore said. "And he was in love with this woman, but he became unglued when he couldn't cut it in school and the girl told him to pack off."

Chapman's experience in Lebanon may have been a factor that contributed to his rapidly destabilizing condition. The tape recording that he had made of the war in the Mideast was evident at that time. Chapman played the tape in Moore's presence on more than one occasion. "He said it was very exciting and he was very scared," is how Moore recalls Chapman's reaction to the tape and to his experiences there.

After his failure at Covenant and his unhappy affair with Jessica, Chapman got a permit in Georgia to carry a gun as a security guard. It is not known if he actually worked at that job.

After that, Chapman split for Hawaii and surfaced at Castle Memorial Hospital, which is located on the island of Oahu. Paul Tharp, the Community Relations Director at Castle Memorial, indicated that Chapman had worked in the hospital's print shop from August 1977 to November 1979. Tharp indicated that Chapman had been hardworking and pleasant with his fellow employees. "He made a lot of friends," Tharp said. "That's why it surprised me when I heard about it."

Chapman's father said that he and his wife visited their son in Hawaii in December of 1977. The elder Chapman recalls the visit as a very happy time for the family. "He took us all over the island," the father said. "Everything was just super."

That visit, with its cheery atmosphere, must have been a tonic for Chapman, who was probably still deeply hurt by his collapsed relationship with Jessica. But that happiness was short-lived. It turned to ashes when he learned of his parents' divorce soon after their return to the mainland in the Atlanta area. Chapman must have depended on his parents for his own emotional stability. Their divorce hard on the heels of the disintegration of his relationship with Jessica was apparently all the impetus he needed to propel him into his first suicide attempt. The method that he chose was carbon monoxide poisoning. Chapman attached a tube to the exhaust system of his automobile and placed it in the window of the passenger compartment. The details of his failure to find death are not available at this time.

David C. Moore didn't see Chapman from the time he left the Fort Chaffee area in early 1977, until Chapman appeared in Geneva, Switzerland, in 1978. Moore was attending conferences at the World Alliance of YMCA's in Geneva. Moore and Chapman spent a good deal of time talking there. Chapman had a lot to say about the troubled time he spent in Hawaii after his break-up with Jessica and the divorce of his parents. "I can remember sitting up on the balcony all night long as he poured out his guts to me about the pressure, mostly about his love life." Moore recalls. "He told me that he had tried to commit suicide in Honolulu, that he had felt life wasn't worth living. He was upset he couldn't establish a good relationship with Jessica and he was devastated by the divorce of his parents because he loved them so much."

Conversations between Moore and Chapman were also the first evidence of some of Chapman's negative feelings toward the Beatles in general and perhaps specifically toward John Lennon. They concerned Lennon's remarks regarding the relative worldwide position of the Beatles and Jesus.

"He was very much a Beatles fan and played their music constantly." Moore recalls. "I can remember one night we had a discussion at home, about the comment by one of the Beatles that they were more important to the world than Jesus Christ.

"I remember him saying, 'Who the hell are they to compare themselves to Jesus?' He harped on it a little. He thought they were being a bit arrogant."

Gregg Lyman talked to Chapman about the Beatles too. "The only conversation Mark and I had about the Beatles was at Fort Chaffee in 1975 over a couple of beers," said Lyman. "Remember, he was very, very religious by then and he said, 'John Lennon shouldn't have said that the Beatles are more important than Jesus Christ.'

"I told him I didn't think it was a big deal, that Lennon could say whatever he likes, and he said, 'No, he shouldn't be that arrogant, it's only going to bring the Beatles harm.'

"But I want to emphasize," Lyman continued, "that he spoke calmly at that time and didn't seem upset."

John Lennon's early career as a solo act aroused a storm of controversy. With wife Yoko Ono, he took a hard anti-war stance.

Before Chapman left on the world tour that brought him to Geneva he had met a Japanese American woman, who worked in a travel agency in Honolulu. Her name was Gloria Abe. She had graduated from Kailua High School in 1969 and had worked in the travel agency since that time. There had been a spark between them. It was Gloria who had planned and booked Chapman's tour. She even went to see him off when he left.

When he returned, he paid a lot of attention to Gloria. They were married on June 2, 1979. It was at the wedding that Gloria first got an idea that something might not be right with Chapman. Reportedly, Chapman would not allow any chairs around and forced the guests to stand at the wedding. He also insisted that there should be no liquor served.

After their marriage, Chapman began to force Gloria to become submissive to him. He insisted that she quit her lucrative job at the travel agency to become a clerk at the hospital where he was working.

It is ironic that both Chapman and his wife ended up working at Castle Memorial, in light of the fact that in 1977 Chapman was a patient at the institution. While at Castle Memorial, Chapman was treated by Dr. Denis Nee Lee, who is now head of the state Mental Health Division.

Chapman suddenly changed jobs. Paul Tharp of Castle Memorial said, "He said he wanted to be above ground because he liked to be in contact with people." Chapman joined up as a security guard with a local company, Freeman Guard Services. He lasted almost a full year with Freeman. During that time he was employed guarding a condominium complex in Honolulu.

Some of Chapman's fellow guards recall him as being nervous. The most bizarre behavior he demonstrated on the job was directed at an equally bizarre institution, the Church of Scientology, which was located across the street from the complex that Chapman guarded. Chapman often shouted abuse at the Scientologists when he saw them in the street. He would also place menacing phone calls to the church, saying over and over: "Bang! Bang! You're dead!" Perhaps he had had an aborted association with the demanding Scientologists.

During that time he began to intensify his identification with the Beatles and especially with Lennon. He played Beatles music constantly in his home and he began to wear the wire-rimmed glasses that are so strongly associated with Lennon. He also began to dress in a style that was like Lennon's.

His bullying of Gloria grew, and Chapman eventually denied her access to newspapers, radio and television. He forced her to give up long-standing social contacts and lifelong friendships.

At that point the couple were living in a high rise building at 55 South Kukui St. in downtown Honolulu. The average price of an apartment in the building is between $400–$450 per month.

Bob Connel, the manager of the complex in which they lived, said that Chapman was a quiet man who enjoyed "paintings and stuff like that." Connel also said that Chapman occasionally bought and sold paintings and was a pretty good amateur guitarist. "He was a very keen painter himself and his ambition was to earn his living as an artist. He seemed to be a lonely man, and he was not very friendly, but there was never any indication that he would turn violent."

A few weeks before he came to New York, Chapman bought a print of a painting by Salvador Dali. Police and psychiatrists have made much of this painting and see it as possibly a key link in reconstructing the thoughts that drove Chapman to his act. Bob Connel remembers that "he was very proud of that painting and it was his most prized possession."

The painting in question is Dali's "Lincoln in Dali Vision" and it portrays the assassination of Lincoln. The shrinks are conjecturing that the painting may have inflamed Chapman's unsteady personality enough to make him think of creating his own grisly masterwork.

Chapman's interest in expensive artwork didn't end with the Dali painting. Gallery experts in Hawaii have revealed that Chapman had spent thousands of dollars on art works. Reportedly, Chapman even bought the Norman Rockwell lithograph "Triple Self Portrait" for $7,500. A Honolulu art sales consultant, Pat Carlson, indicated that Chapman borrowed money to support his art habit.

This is one of the mysterious elements that have not been satisfactorily explained. Chapman was a security guard who lived in a $400-a-month apartment, which he filled with expensive art work, even though he earned only about $4.00 an hour. He was also found with over two thousand dollars in cash when he was arrested in New York. It's easy to say, 'He borrowed money for the paintings,' or 'He took a loan from a credit union to get to New York.' Somehow it doesn't wash. There has to be something else.

Events began to draw near the climax. On Nov. 23, 1980, Chapman quit his job, but he didn't do it in an ordinary way. In speaking to the man who took over Chapman's guard duties, Mike Bird, Chapman said he had to leave to go to London, England. It's obvious that he had the English-born Lennon on his mind then. An even stranger event occurred a short time later. "The last day he worked," Mike Bird relates, "he signed 'John Lennon' instead of Mark Chapman on the Log." It is also known that Chapman pasted Lennon's name over his own on the nameplate of his guard uniform.

These events led to a wave of speculation by psychiatrists and the media that Chapman may have lost or submerged his identity in Lennon's as a result of the personality disturbances that he suffered. Some of these 'experts' see the shooting of Lennon as an act of psychological 'suicide' by Chapman. They see Chapman's act of signing the logbook with Lennon's name as an indication that he was beginning to lose his own identity. New York psychiatrist David Abrahamsen said, "Signing John Lennon's name possibly meant that he somehow identified himself with Lennon. It is very strange and indicates that he was quite ill."

Stuart Berger, a former professor of legal psychiatry at Harvard, said this: "There can be such a psychotic loss of ego boundaries with the victim so that the murderer almost perceives himself as one with the victim, and ultimately he *is* the victim."

Other psychologists have said that this case in

some ways resembles family tragedies where a son kills his father because the son sees himself as the head of the family and can only assume that role if the real head of the family is eliminated.

"You shoot them so you can be them. It is an act of primitive deranged thinking, where the murderer believes at one level that by eliminating the victim he can become the victim." said Dr. Berger.

In a further rumination on the danger of the loss of ego boundaries, which in many cases leads to an identification with celebrities, Dr. Berger continues to comment on Chapman. "What appears in particular from the speculative evidence is the emptiness, frustration, anger and failure this man has experienced over his lifetime. It culminates in a premeditated and coherent attack on Lennon, whom he perceives as a man he would have liked to have been."

David Abrahamsen sums it up in this manner. "On the one side he wants to kill himself, and on the other side he wants to kill off someone like John Lennon. If Chapman identified so much with Lennon, he could have had a grudge against Lennon because he (Chapman) didn't get as far as Lennon."

On October 27, 1980, four days after signing Lennon's name to his security job logbook, Chapman walked into a shop in downtown Honolulu, J & S Enterprises—Guns. Chapman purchased for $169 a .38-caliber Charter Arms Undercover Special, a weapon which is sometimes carried by detectives and off-duty policemen. Arthur Bremer used the same model when he gunned down George Wallace in suburban Maryland. Charter Arms Corp. of Stratford, Connecticut is the company that makes the deadly .44-caliber 'Bulldog' revolver that Son of Sam killer David Berkowitz used on his victims.

According to Honolulu police, Chapman applied for a permit earlier in October. Chapman cited an alleged burglary at his home in August as the reason for wanting a pistol. The check on Chapman showed nothing negative, so he was issued a 'premises permit,' which allows the gun-owner to keep the weapon in his home or place of business, but does not allow him to carry it about. According to Hawaii's law, which is like the law in New York City, the permittee must be an American citizen, must be at least twenty years old, must not have a criminal record or any history of time in a mental institution and must not have been discharged dishonorably from the armed forces. Reports that Chapman spent time in an Hawaiian mental institution must be born in mind when considering the ease with which Chapman was able to get his permit.

The Undercover Special is a snub-nosed, five-chambered gun. The weapon has the advantage of being very light (it weighs about a pound); it has a short barrel which is either two or three inches long. Its small size makes it perfect for use as a concealed weapon.

In order to penetrate a human being, a bullet must travel at a velocity of approximately 300 feet per second; the Undercover Special is an accurate weapon that discharges rounds at a velocity of 700 to 750 feet per second and the rounds hold that velocity for distances up to fifty feet.

Since the assassination, J&S Enterprises has received numerous threats of destruction. In defense of himself and his business, Steve Grahovac said, in what may have been an attempt at grisly humor, "We do a bang-up business. I may have seen him here, but I didn't see him make the purchase.

"You cannot analyze everyone. We are not doctors, but if there had been anything weird in his manner when he came into the store, the gun would not have been sold to him.

"I can tell you this," Grahovac continued lamely, "if a guy starts talking weird, saying he's going to shoot someone, then we won't sell him the gun." Thanks, Steve, that's real civic-minded of you!

Some time after he purchased the gun, Chapman told his wife, "I'm going to New York and make it all different."

Officials at the Makiki Mental Health Clinic say that on Nov. 20, 1980 Chapman got in touch with their hotline and reportedly sounded "under stress." Makiki referred Chapman to Catholic Social Services, which is an organization that provides psychological counseling and therapy.

Catholic Social Services Director Robert Omura said that Chapman's call was taken by a social worker. "He felt that Mr. Chapman was under stress, sounding a little depressed, but coherent and mentally alert. The social worker offered Chapman an appointment time." Chapman responded that he could come in almost any time because he was unemployed. The social worker gave him an appointment on the twenty-sixth of November. Chapman never showed, and the social worker tried to locate him repeatedly right up until the day John Lennon was shot.

According to an airplane ticket that belonged to Chapman, it was determined that he arrived in New York Saturday, December sixth. Chapman was seen lurking outside the Dakota on that day, so it seems that he began stalking Lennon as soon as he got to New York.

Chapman registered at a place that must have filled him with disturbing associations—the YMCA at 5 West 63rd Street, a few blocks south of the Dakota which is located at 72nd. Chapman showed his Hawaiian license and gave his proper address. He gave the clerk three days rent in advance, $49.50, and was given the key for room 1041.

Chapman then apparently took a series of cab rides around Manhattan's Greenwich Village and Upper West Side. During one of these rides, Chapman reportedly claimed to be a sound engineer for Lennon and that he had to deliver cassette tapes from recent recording sessions to various locations around town. Chapman allegedly offered cocaine and other drugs to the cabdriver.

On Sunday, December seventh, Chapman somehow managed to meet up with Sean Lennon's babysitter and had a meal with her. The babysitter found him to be pleasant. He also decided to change hotels that day and went somewhat farther downtown to the more posh Sheraton Center Hotel, located on 52nd St. and Seventh Ave. He was assigned room 2730, planning to pay the $82-a-day bill with a credit card. Chapman returned to the Dakota. Later that evening he returned to the Sheraton and charged an expensive meal before going to sleep.

Monday, December eighth at approximately

12:30 PM, Chapman, in a brown coat and imitation fur hat, was back outside the Dakota. He stood near the entrance for a short while before deciding to approach another young man with a camera, who was also lingering in the area. Chapman walked up to Paul Goresh, a freelance photographer, and asked, "You waiting for Lennon?" Goresh replied, "Yeah. Where are you from?" Chapman said he was from Hawaii, but when Goresh asked Chapman where he was staying while he was in town, Chapman became slightly surly and defensive. At that point Goresh stepped away so as not to precipitate any kind of hassle. After a slight hesitation, Chapman walked over to Goresh and apologized for his behavior saying, "I didn't mean to insult you. You know, you can't be too careful these days." Around 5:00 PM Lennon left the Dakota. Yoko Ono accompanied him. When Lennon stepped out on the sidewalk, Chapman held out a copy of John and Yoko's new album, *Double Fantasy*; Lennon took the pen that Chapman offered and autographed the album jacket for Chapman. Chapman stood behind Lennon's shoulder and watched. Goresh snapped a picture of the event.

Lennon asked Chapman, "Is that okay? Is that what you want?" Lennon left and Chapman excitedly asked Goresh, "Did I have my hat on or off in the picture? I wanted my hat off. They'll never believe this in Hawaii."

The two men killed time separately for a few hours. Around 7:45 PM, Goresh decided that he'd had enough and told Chapman that he was going to leave. Chapman wanted Goresh to stay, and tried to convince him by saying, "You never

Look-alike John and Yoko at their charity art show in London.

know; something might happen; you know, he could go to Spain or something tonight and you might never see him again."

Goresh left and some time after that Chapman must also have left the Dakota and returned to the room at the Sheraton Center, because the autographed album was found there in room 2730 when the police searched it after Chapman's apprehension.

The Lennons spent several hours at The Record Plant sound studio on West 44th Street with their friends and producers, Jack Douglas and David Geffen. They were supervising the transfer of album cuts into singles format. When they were finished, John and Yoko said they were going to stop and grab something to eat before going home. They arrived at the Dakota at approximately 10:50 PM. Their limousine pulled up at the curb rather than pulling into the Dakota's courtyard. Lennon and Yoko stepped out of the car and walked toward the Gothic archway that graces the entrance of the Dakota. Chapman was lurking just inside the archway and when Lennon had passed, Chapman dropped into a combat crouch, with both arms outstretched, both hands steadying the pistol. He emptied the pistol, pumping four slugs into Lennon's back, two in the left side of the back and two into his left shoulder.

An eyewitness, Lennon's neighbor Ellen Chesler, 33, described the chilling event this way: "Lennon's car left him off at the curb and he walked into the courtyard. He turned right, to an office where he walks in to take the elevator to his part of the building. He was hit as he was turning to walk inside. The guy was sort of following him in. I watched the whole thing from my window. I was sitting in the rocking chair with my baby in my arms.

"I didn't hear any screams. He called out, 'Mr. Lennon!' and he (Lennon) kept walking and he got it right in the back. I watched him fall down. I heard four shots. The shots echoed through the courtyard in the building.

"I saw people scurrying about and they were dragging his body in. The guy just stood there and dropped his gun and Yoko was there with John. The police were there within four minutes.

"It's just unbelievable. He very rarely went out. His son goes to nursery school with my son. It's very, very tragic. To the rest of the world it's John Lennon, but if you live in the building it's a neighbor.

"There's something about witnessing a murder," Chesler continued. "Even if it's within your own apartment. I feel so bad about it, I'm still not settled."

After shooting Lennon, Chapman apparently dropped the gun where he stood. Dakota employees kicked the gun away from him, and asked him if he knew what he'd done. Chapman reportedly said, "Yes, I killed John Lennon." Then Chapman reportedly took a copy of *Catcher in the Rye* out of his pocket, sat down and began to read. The police arrived on the scene in minutes. They tried resuscitation techniques, but then decided that Lennon's condition was so grave that they had to take him immediately to a hospital without waiting for an ambulance. They placed Lennon in the back seat of a police cruiser and sped away to Roosevelt Hospital. Lennon was apparently still alive at the outset of the ride because the police officer asked him if he was John Lennon and Lennon reportedly nodded and groaned. Yoko Ono was in another cruiser close behind.

The policemen radioed ahead to Roosevelt Hospital, located at 60th Street and Eighth Avenue, and by the time they arrived emergency crews were on hand waiting.

After Lennon had been rushed away, the police hustled Chapman, who now had his hands manacled behind his back, into a police car. One witness said that Chapman was scuffling with the police at that point. Chapman also asked the cops to pick up his book which he had dropped to the ground. He reportedly said, "I'm afraid, don't let them hurt me," and "I didn't have any reason to kill him."

He was taken to the 82nd Street station house where he was held until the following morning, when he was brought to the Criminal Court Building, before Judge Martin Rettinger. On Tuesday, December ninth, Judge Rettinger charged Chapman with second degree murder and unlawful possession of the murder weapon. He ordered Chapman sent to Manhattan's Bellevue Hospital for thirty days of psychiatric observation under a "suicide watch." The suicide watch meant that Chapman would have to be physically observed at least once every fifteen minutes and accompanied everywhere he went outside of his cell.

The scene at Bellevue on Manhattan's East Side was completely chaotic. When hospital officials were informed that Chapman was to be held in their psychiatric ward, they panicked. They pleaded with police to first bring Chapman to the city's other secure psychiatric facility, Kings County General Hospital, so that he could be transferred in the dead of night to Bellevue with as little fanfare as possible. The officials at Bellevue were not concerned without reason. The facility was immediately filled with all kinds of people milling about. Most of the huge crowd that filled the corridors were from the press, but the Bellevue staff did not have time to set up the elaborate security precautions that have since become the rule in dealing with Chapman. The hospital switchboard was already lighting up with death threats and Bellevue officials were frightened that a potential killer intent on revenge for the Lennon killing might have already slipped into the seething crowd.

The police were unwilling to transport Chapman out to Brooklyn and apparently wanted to get him into a secure facility immediately so that they could regroup and plan their precautions.

Another incident muddied up the story of Chapman. The news was released that Chapman had a long criminal record prior to Lennon's shooting. Only an hour or so after that news had been flashed around the world, another announcement denied the earlier report and the information was given that Chapman actually had no criminal record.

Investigators entered Chapman's room at the Sheraton Center and found a number of his possessions there: his personal Bible; a placemat decorated with a tableau from the *Wizard of Oz* movie, showing Judy Garland standing with the Scarecrow, the Tin Man and the Cowardly Lion;

At the Grammy Awards held at the Uris Theatre in New York City, in March of 1975. From left are: David Bowie, Art Garfunkel, Paul Simon, Yoko Ono, John Lennon and Roberta Flack.

and the one-way ticket that had brought him there from Hawaii. The accused's expired passport, an introductory letter from the YMCA and some photos of Chapman were also found. The strangest thing was an eight track tape of an album by Todd Rundgren. What makes it so bizarre is that six years ago Chapman sent a cassette tape to a friend, Miles McManus, which begins with Chapman saying, "Hello and welcome to the Mark Chapman tape." Chapman had written a borrowed title on the outside of the tape, "Portrait of a Crazy Man." The title is borrowed from the first line of the Rundgren song "An Elpee's Worth of Toons" which Chapman stated, in a monologue on the tape, moved him to tears. When McManus realized that the Chapman involved in Lennon's death was the same one who had sent him the tape, he retrieved it and said, "I couldn't believe it. When I saw the title of the tape, I had forgotten what he wrote on the tape, and when I played it I just started crying."

Chapman reportedly told guards at Bellevue, "I've got a good side and a bad side. The bad side is very small but sometimes it takes over the good side and I do bad things."

On Thursday, December eleventh, the police set up a special team of detectives who were assigned to deal with the ever-increasing flood of death threats to anyone who had anything to do with the Chapman case. One detective had this to say: "There are a lot of crazies who phone in. The calls started moments after word of the killing spread.

"You tend to want to ignore them, but can you imagine how many heads would roll if there's another Jack Ruby out there (Ruby was the man who murdered President Kennedy's alleged assassin, Lee Harvey Oswald, while Oswald was in police custody) and we let him succeed?''

The threats continued to accelerate and Chapman's lawyer, Herbert Adlerberg, resigned. The 50-year-old lawyer's face was dead white when he made his statement. ''Everyone in the case will be marked for death if he is found not guilty by reason of insanity,'' Adlerberg said. ''I'm really scared. I know I'm throwing away the biggest case of my career, but I don't want it to be the last case I handle.''

Adlerberg repeated that he felt everyone would be a target for rage. ''That includes Criminal Court Judge Martin Rettinger, Assistant District Attorney Allen Sullivan and Jonathan Marks, who took over for me when I resigned.

''I know I'm a quitter like Roberto Duran, but I'm doing it for my family. If I were a younger man and single, I'd see this through.''

Adlerberg believes that the adoration of Lennon is ''a cult thing'' and very volatile. ''It has international ramifications. I'm scared that I and my family will be killed.''

During his stay at Bellevue, Chapman showed no interest in reading or watching television; reportedly he spent most of his time staring at the ceiling. Because he was on suicide watch, his belt and shoelaces had been removed and there were no pipes or bars in the room from which he could hang himself.

Saturday, December thirteenth, Chapman was moved from Bellevue Hospital to a green Correction Department bus at 4:45 PM. Six police cars with sirens wailing escorted the bus on the forty-minute trip to the medical and psychiatric building at the Rikers Island Prison.

A Correction Department spokesman said, "The feeling is that he would be safer on Rikers; for one thing, there is only one bridge leading to Rikers and Bellevue is in the middle of Manhattan. It's just easier to keep people away from Rikers than from Bellevue."

Chapman was housed in a section of the infirmary that normally holds up to two dozen inmates. Twelve to fifteen prisoners were moved out to ensure that Chapman could be kept safely in total isolation. It was a sound idea; one of the inmates left a death threat scrawled on the wall of the room. The threat which misspelled Chapman's name and several other words reportedly read: "Champlian. You have not much time laft. Don't feel pity. Now it is behind that?"

This death threat inspired a fear in Chapman that the inmates who carry food to isolated prisoners would poison him. He went on a hunger strike right away.

Jonathan Marks, the lawyer who took over Chapman's defense from Adlerberg, decided that Chapman should enter a plea of insanity to the charge of second-degree murder that has been lodged against him. "Mark Chapman desperately needs a friend. This man is very much alone. The whole world is against him," Marks began in a partial explanation of why he took the Chapman case. "The death of John Lennon is a great tragedy that has aroused emotions around the world.

"Obviously, Mark Chapman's mental state is a critical issue in this case. Insanity is a defense, while in order to convict, the prosecution must show criminal intent."

On Sunday, December fourteenth, Marks convinced Chapman to end his hunger strike by having civilians rather than prisoners bring him the food. It was only hours after the vigil in New York's Central Park, when almost two hundred thousand people stood silently in the park and thought of John Lennon, while millions watched.

For reasons of security, the police, the courts and Chapman's lawyer tried desperately to keep Lennon's death from turning into a circus. Lurid newspaper headlines were disturbing, but there were other events that were more distressing.

The fact that Chapman was able to purchase so easily the pistol that he used, is not easy to accept. Chapman was a man who had a history of mental instability. Hawaii's gun law stipulates that anyone who has spent time in a mental institution cannot be issued a permit to purchase a handgun. The Honolulu police could not have performed a very thorough check on Chapman, if they did not find his history of psychological problems, especially since he was treated at Castle Memorial Hospital which is in Honolulu.

Guns can be smuggled through the metal detectors and x-ray baggage scans at the airports. Had the pistol been detected at the airport, tragedy might have been prevented.

In the confusion and hail of rumor that surrounded the case, the fact that the authorities allowed an erroneous statement get publicized and add to the confusion is almost unpardonable. The statement is the one which tagged Chapman with an extensive criminal record. The fact that the statement was retracted not long afterward with the scarcely satisfactory explanation that Chapman had been mistaken for someone who was "probably" incarcerated "somewhere" in Ohio, is secondary.

A vital piece of evidence, the *Double Fantasy* album that Lennon autographed for Chapman which was found in a search of Chapman's Sheraton Center hotel room, mysteriously disappeared from police custody. The brief explanation was that a "fan" had probably stolen it, and it was stated that the police hoped that they would be able to get it back. That album was important in establishing some of Chapman's movements after he was last seen by Paul Goresh. It is incredible that the album was lost.

The resignation of Chapman's first lawyer, Alderberg, on account of death threats added to the reigning confusion and uneasiness.

Perhaps the extent of the emotional reaction of the world to Lennon's death and the intensity of it in New York created such pressure on the system that it could not help faltering.

When Lennon had been trying to enter the United States, he had to fight tooth and nail with immigration officials. The pretext for refusing him was a minor infraction involving a small amount of hash; in many parts of the United States it is no longer a crime, but at that time Lennon was guilty.

He was a highly visible, world-renowned figure and very vocal in his resistance to America's involvement in the Vietnam War. Senator Strom Thurmond, from South Carolina, was the force behind Lennon's problems with immigration.

After Lennon won his case, he remained silent

for five years. He spoke publicaly only to deny rumors of imminent Beatle reunifications. Some critics complained that he was afraid of the heat from the establishment that at one point threatened to keep him out of the United States. Perhaps they were right, and if they were, perhaps Lennon was right to be afraid.

That period of silence had recently ended. Lennon's joint musical effort with Yoko Ono signified that he was about to resurface. He had already done extensive talking in the print media, notably a *Playboy* interview. He had also appeared on radio and television. Lennon was about to become a public figure again.

A widespread initial reaction to the news of Lennon's death was a sardonic one; it claimed Lennon's death as a fitting way to begin the Reagan administration.

People also likened Lennon's demise to the Kennedy assassinations and to Lincoln's and that of Martin Luther King. Of course, those are the obvious ones. What is most disturbing is that Americans can refer to a list like this. We are becoming accustomed to having our political symbols snuffed out, especially the positive ones. It is hard to differentiate between the long list of "crazed, lone gunmen" and the spiritual and political climate in America that is so conducive to violent tragedy.

In an early morning phone call to the police, Gloria Chapman's first words on the horrible event were, "Please help him. He's sick. He needs help." A few days later she said that she felt a "great sadness" and that she hoped America and the rest of the world could forgive Chapman. "I'm very sorry this has happened," she said. "I'm very sorry that John Lennon has died and his wife and son are suffering."

She also said, "As a Christian, I believe forgiveness is a very important thing," and that she was hoping that "somehow, some good is going to come out of this."

Chapman's father, who works for the Citizens and Southern National Bank, has not attempted to visit or talk with his son. When asked for his comments, the elder Chapman decided to let the press transmit a message for him.

"The bank has asked me to keep a low profile," he began. "I would certainly like to wish him—whatever. It's hard to know what to say."

Chronology

1940
October 9th: John Winston Lennon, son of Alfred and Julia Lennon, is born at 7:00 A.M. at Oxford Maternity Hospital in Liverpool.

1943–51   Alfred Lennon disappears for a time; Julia is left without support. John lives first with his mother, then briefly with his father, and finally ends up with his mother's sister Mimi and her husband George. John attends Dovedale Primary School and proves a precocious child.

1952   John starts Quarry Bank High School; he is known as the class cut-up. He develops an interest in art and writing.

1953–55   Mimi's husband George dies; influence of mother Julia becomes stronger in John's life. Despite troubles in school, an interested teacher recognizes his talent in art.

1956   John first hears Elvis' *Heartbreak Hotel*. His mother encourages his musical interest and buys him his first guitar for ten pounds. John forms the Quarrymen.

1957   John starts school at the Liverpool College of Art; meets his future wife Cynthia Powell, a classmate in his Lettering section. On June 15th, he meets Paul McCartney. John and Paul perform as the "Nurk Twins."

1958   Julia Lennon is killed in a car accident. John meets George Harrison.

1959   Quarrymen play at the opening of the Casbah, a club in the basement at the home of Pete Best. Stu Sutcliffe joins the group. John renames the band the "Silver Beatles." They tour Scotland using their pseudonyms: Paul Ramon, Johnny Silver, Stu de Stijl and Carl Harrison and a drummer named

Thomas Moore. Quarrymen replace Moore with Pete Best.

1960–61
The group now known just as the Beatles is considered one of the top bands in Liverpool. Members are John, Paul, George, Stu Sutcliffe and Pete Best. They make several trips to Hamburg and develop their raw, exciting sound. The Beatles meet Klaus Voormann and Astrid Kirchherr, who influence their clothing and hairstyle. Beatles record "My Bonnie."

October, 1961:
Beatles meet Brian Epstein, who becomes their manager.

1962
January 1st:
First audition with major label, Decca. Later, they win a *Mersey Beat* poll as the most popular group in Liverpool.

April:
Stu Sutcliffe dies of a brain hemorrhage. Return to Germany for another Hamburg tour, where they meet Ringo Starr.

August:
Pete Best is sacked and Ringo hired.

August 23rd:	John and Cynthia are married at the Mount Pleasant Register Office, Liverpool.
September 11th:	"Love Me Do" is recorded at EMI. It sells 10,000 copies the first week of its release.
November:	First T. V. appearance on "People and Places."
December:	A last trip to Hamburg.

1963
February: Beatles make nationwide tour of U.K.

February 16th: "Please Please Me" hits No. 1 on the charts.

December 29th: "I Want To Hold Your Hand" first broadcast on WMCA, New York City. John's son Julian born.

1964   First LP *Meet the Beatles* is cut in sixteen hours. The group plays a brief engagement in France.

MERSEY BEAT

Beatles Top Poll!

In the beginning of 1962 the Beatles, with Pete Best still included, won the Mersey Beat poll. Note that Best still refused to comb his hair down in true Beatle fashion. Also, the ad in the upper right corner is for Brian's stores.

Beatles as they looked after adopting Brian's law—that they look absolutely neat at all performances. . . .

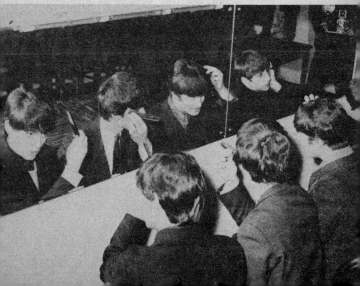

February 7th:	Arrive at Kennedy Airport in New York for their first American engagements. The Beatles appear on the "Ed Sullivan Show" and play at Carnegie Hall in New York before 2,900 screaming fans. Next stop: Washington. Filming for *A Hard Day's Night* begins.
March 23rd:	John's book *In His Own Write* is published; it wins the prestigious Foyle's literary prize.
March 31st:	U.S. *Billboard* top 100 chart: No. 1: "Can't Buy Me Love;" No. 2: "Twist and Shout;" No. 3: "She Loves You;" No. 4: "I Want To Hold Your Hand;" No. 5: "Please Please Me;" and numbers 16, 44, 49, 69, 78, 84 and 88 also Beatles songs.
April:	Second album released
May 6th:	"Around the Beatles" T.V. show aired.
June:	*A Hard Day's Night* LP appears.
July 6th:	Royal premiere of film *A Hard*

Day's Night. Also in July, *Some-thing New* album released.

August 19th-September 20th:	Second U.S. visit.
October-November:	Tour with Mary Wells in England.
December:	"Another Beatles Christmas Show."

1965
January:	Albums *Beatles Story* and *Beatles '65* released. George and John are introduced to LSD.
February 22nd:	Beatles begin filming of movie *Help.*
March:	*Early Beatles* album released; also, *Beatles IV.*
June 12th:	Announcement that the Beatles will be awarded the MBE. Also in June, John's second book, *A Spaniard in the Works*, is published.
July 29th:	*Help* premieres at the London Pavillion.

August:	*Help* LP released.
August 15th:	Beatles return to America and play to 55,000 people at Shea Stadium in New York. The tour also included more taping for the "Ed Sullivan Show." Later, the Fab Four are vested with MBEs. They smoke a joint in the bathroom at Buckingham Palace.
December:	Release of *Rubber Soul* LP. Last tour of England; Moody Blues play the opening act. *New Musical Express* poll winners.

1966
June:	*Yesterday and Today* released.
June 30–July 2:	Japan tour.
August:	LP *Revolver* released.
August 12–29th:	Last American tour starts in Chicago and ends in San Francisco. John makes his "bigger than Jesus" statement, which causes great controversy. After tours, John meets Yoko at a London gallery.

September-October:	John makes his solo film debut in Richard Lester's *How I Won The War*.
December:	Begin recording *Sgt. Pepper's Lonely Hearts Club Band*.

1967

A reconciliation is affected between John and Fred Lennon. John puts his dad on his personal payroll.

June 1st:	Release of *Sgt. Pepper*. Controversy rages over illicit drug references. That month, George Harrison meets the Maharishi Mahesh Yogi. Group decides to retire from touring completely and begins to concentrate their energies in the studio. "Penny Lane" and "Strawberry Fields" fail to make No. 1 on the charts.
June 25th:	Appear on "Our World," international live T.V. show. Shows Beatles recording "All You Need Is Love" and "Baby You're A Rich Man."
August 27th:	Brian Epstein dies of an overdose of barbiturates. Beatles hear the news while meeting with the Maharishi in Wales. Later, they make the color T.V. film *Magical Mystery Tour*.

December 7th:	Grand opening of the Beatles Apple Boutique at 94 Baker Street, London. Also that month, *MMT* LP released.
December 26th:	World premiere on BBC-TV of *Magical Mystery Tour* show.

1968

January 5th:	*MMT* shown for second time on BBC.
February:	Apple Corps, Ltd. founded. It is the parent company for the boutique, Apple Electronics, Apple Music Publishing and Apple Films, Ltd. Beatles later stay at the Maharishi's Academy in Rishikesh, India.
July:	Due to poor management, Apple Boutique closes after seven months. World premiere of *Yellow Submarine* at the London Pavillion.
August 28th:	"Hey Jude," the first Apple record, is released.
October 19th:	John and Yoko are busted.
November 8th:	John and Cynthia divorce. Cynthia names Yoko as "the other woman."

November:	Release of *The Beatles* ("White Album") and of John and Yoko's *Two Virgins*. Former shows nothing on the cover; latter shows John and Yoko wearing nothing on the cover.
1969 *January:*	Work begins on *Let It Be*. January 30th, the Beatles perform a free lunchtime concert on the roof of Apple. They record "Get Back."
February:	*Yellow Submarine* LP released. John and Yoko married on Gibraltar. Begin their honeymoon at the Amsterdam Hilton in a seven-day bed-in for peace. John changes his name to John Ono Lennon in a ceremony on the roof of Apple headquarters. Later that year, John releases a solo LP, *Unfinished Music No. 2: Life With the Lions*.
June:	Allen Klein starts managing the Beatles.
October:	Apple *Abbey Road* recorded. It is the last album the Beatles record as a unit.
November:	John and Yoko release *The Wedding Album*, which they recorded in October.

November 25th:	John returns his MBE "with love" to the Queen. He protests Britain's involvement in Biafra and Viet Nam.
December:	Release of John and Yoko's *The Plastic Ono Band Live Peace in Toronto*. It is the first time a Beatle forms and plays with another group. John, Yoko, George and Delaney and Bonnie jam at a "War Is Over" concert at the Lyceum.

1970

January 14th:	John's erotic lithographs exhibited at a London gallery. The show is closed for a few days while eight prints are removed for possible prosecution under the Obscene Publications Act.
January 25th:	John and Yoko have their heads cropped and declare it to be the "Year One."
January 27th:	John records *Instant Karma* with Phil Spector.
February 26th:	*Hey Jude*, a collection of singles which had not previously been on albums, is released.
April 10th:	Beatles official break-up.

In December of 1966, John Lennon made a two minute appearance as a doorman on a British TV comedy. Here, he shows style.

April 27th:	John's lithos are handed back because they are unlikely to deprave or corrupt.
July 31st:	Cynthia Lennon marries Roberto Bassanini.
December 11th:	Release of *John Lennon/Plastic Ono Band*.

1971
January 1st:

	Paul McCartney sets about legally to dissolve connections with the Beatles and their company.
March 3rd:	South Africa lifts a five-year ban on the Beatles.
March 12th:	A receiver is appointed in the Beatles litigation. John, George and Ringo appeal on March 17th.
December 11th:	John and Yoko participate in the John Sinclair Ann Arbor Benefit.

1972
February:

	The Beatles fan club liquidates its shop.
August 31st:	John and Yoko, Elephant's Mem-

ory, and an all-star bill stage a charity show for mentally retarded children at Madison Square Garden. The show is called "One-to-One."

1973
February: Rumors spread that John and Yoko's marriage is rocky. "We're facing a lot of problems," says Yoko.

March: Late in the month, John, Paul and Ringo terminate their contract with Allen Klein. Through the next months, repackaging of Beatles material begins.

July 10th: Release of Ringo's LP *Ringo*.

October 2nd: John and Yoko go to Los Angeles.

November: John, Paul and Ringo sue Allen Klein. John releases "Mind Games."

1974
January: John asks the Queen for a Royal pardon in connection with his drug conviction, so that he will be free to travel to and from the United States.

February:	Reports that John and Yoko have split. John physically ejected from the Troubadour Club after creating a disturbance.
March:	John ordered to leave the U.S. Yoko wins custody of her daughter Kyoko. Her former husband Anthony Cox kidnaps their child. For the first time in four years, John, Ringo and George record a Lennon tune, "I Am The Greatest."
April 1st:	Release of *Beatles 1962–66* and *Beatles 1967–70*.
July 17th:	John is ordered to leave the U.S. by the Department of Justice. He begins appealing the ruling—which ends up taking years to resolve.
September:	The Board of Immigration Appeals orders John to leave the U.S. or be deported. John lodges another appeal.
1975 *January:*	The Beatles partnership is legally dissolved. John records with the Elton John Band a successful reworking of "I Saw Her Standing There."

September:	Yoko is pregnant with John's second son Sean. Because of this, the U.S. Immigration and Naturalization Service grants John a temporary non-priority status.
October 7th:	The U.S. Court of Appeals overturns the order to deport John.
October 9th:	John and Yoko announce the happy news of the birth of Sean—the same date as John's birthday.
October 24th:	Release of *Shaved Fish (Collectable Lennon)* produced by John, Yoko and Phil Spector. Also released on this date are the four-year-old *Imagine* and the single "Working Class Hero."
1976–80	John lives in relative obscurity with his family in his apartment in the Dakota, on New York's Upper West Side.
1980 *November:*	John releases his comeback album with Yoko, *Double Fantasy*.
December 8th:	John Ono Lennon is shot to death in front of his home by a "fan," Mark David Chapman.

December 14th: A worldwide vigil is held. There are ten minutes of silence for a man who had dedicated his life to music, love and peace.